SUPER EASY
BLACKSTONE
OUTDOOR GAS GRIDDLE
COOKBOOK

Dive into Gourmet Grilling with 2000+ Days of Exquisite
American Recipes for Every Season

Expert Tips Included

JAKE CHASEY

Table of Contents

Preface

Welcome to the captivating world of outdoor griddle cooking, a method that seamlessly blends simplicity with sophistication, turning every meal into a celebration. This book is crafted with both the novice and seasoned chef in mind, aiming to unfold the countless joys and undeniable benefits of cooking with a Blackstone gas griddle. Whether your kitchen is under the vast sky or a backyard roof, this guide promises to transform your culinary experience by introducing a fresh, flavorful approach to everyday cooking.

The Blackstone gas griddle isn't just another cooking appliance; it's a gateway to exploring gourmet grilling with an ease and versatility that stands unmatched. Designed for chefs of all levels, it offers a substantial cooking surface, robust durability, and precise temperature control, making it a top choice for those who cherish the art of cooking outdoors. Its thoughtful features, from easy assembly to an efficient grease management system, ensure that every cooking session is as enjoyable as it is delicious.

In this preface, we embark on a journey that covers not only the basics of griddle cooking but also dives deep into the myriad benefits it brings. From hosting vibrant gatherings to preparing quiet, intimate family meals, the Blackstone griddle adapts to all occasions, enhancing flavors and forging unforgettable dining experiences. This guide is packed with expert advice, practical tips, and more than two thousand days' worth of recipes that cater to every season and palate. Each recipe is crafted to showcase the griddle's capability to enhance the natural flavors of the ingredients while offering a visually appealing and satisfying meal.

As we move forward, you will find detailed chapters on mastering your Blackstone gas griddle, complete with step-by-step instructions on setup, maintenance, and cooking techniques. These initial sections are designed to build your confidence, ensuring that you can harness the full potential of your griddle with ease. Following the fundamentals, the cookbook unfolds into a diverse collection of recipes—from quick weekday meals to elaborate feasts designed for gatherings—all of which can be prepared on your Blackstone griddle.

This book is more than just a collection of recipes; it is a comprehensive guide to transforming your approach to outdoor cooking, making every meal an opportunity to create something extraordinary. Whether you are a griddle novice eager to learn the basics or an experienced chef looking to expand your culinary repertoire, this guide is your essential companion. Let's heat up the griddle and start this flavorful journey together, exploring the endless possibilities that outdoor griddle cooking has to offer.

Part I: Mastering Your Blackstone Gas Griddle

Chapter 1: Getting Started with Your Blackstone Griddle

Understanding Your Griddle: Components, Setup, and Initial Seasoning

Embarking on your culinary adventure with the Blackstone gas griddle begins with understanding its robust design and functionality. The heart of your setup is the griddle top, a large, flat cooking surface made from cold-rolled steel that distributes heat evenly. This surface sits atop multiple adjustable burners that provide the heat, controlled by knobs that allow you to manage different cooking temperatures across the griddle. The unit is supported by sturdy legs and often includes shelving for convenient storage of tools and ingredients. The essential grease management system facilitates easy cleanup and safe cooking.

Setting up your Blackstone griddle is straightforward. Start by assembling the base, attaching the legs and shelves according to the manufacturer's instructions. Carefully place the griddle top on the frame, ensuring it's properly aligned and secure. Then, connect the griddle to a propane tank or a natural gas line, based on your model's specifications, always checking for gas leaks with a soapy water solution to ensure safety before use. Before cooking for the first time, the griddle top must be seasoned to create a non-stick surface and protect it from rust. This involves heating the clean griddle top, applying a high smoke point oil evenly across its surface, and allowing it to bake in until it polymerizes, forming a durable protective layer.

Safety First: Basic Safety Tips for Outdoor Gas Griddle Use

Safety is crucial when operating your Blackstone gas griddle, ensuring that each cooking experience is both enjoyable and secure. Choose a well-ventilated, open area for your griddle setup to avoid the buildup of harmful gases and ensure it is away from flammable materials. Regularly check for gas leaks, particularly if the griddle has been inactive, by applying a soap solution along the gas lines and watching for bubbles that indicate a leak.

Lighting the griddle should always be done with the lid open to prevent gas accumulation and potential flare-ups. Use the built-in ignition for convenience or a long match or lighter if manual lighting is necessary. Opt for long-handled, heat-resistant utensils to maintain a safe distance from the hot cooking surface.

Maintaining your griddle is key to safe operation. Clean the griddle after each use and perform regular checks on the burners and grease trap to prevent clogs and ensure optimal functionality. Have a fire extinguisher appropriate for grease fires nearby in case of emergencies and never leave a hot griddle unattended. Always supervise the cooking area, especially around children and pets, to avoid accidents.

By adhering to these safety practices, you can maximize the performance of your Blackstone griddle and enjoy a multitude of delicious, safely-prepared meals. This foundation will not only prolong the life of your griddle but also enhance your cooking experience, making every meal a delightful culinary journey.

Chapter 2: The Basics of Griddle Cooking

Temperature Management: How to Control Heat for Different Dishes

Effective temperature management is a cornerstone of successful griddle cooking. The Blackstone gas griddle offers precise control over heat, which is essential for cooking a variety of dishes to perfection. Understanding how to manipulate these temperatures allows you to expand your culinary repertoire, from delicate breakfast items to robust dinner feasts.

The Blackstone griddle is equipped with multiple burners, typically ranging from two to four, depending on the model. Each burner can be controlled independently, providing the ability to create distinct heat zones across the griddle surface. This feature is particularly useful when preparing multiple dishes simultaneously or when a single dish requires different temperatures during cooking.

For beginners, it's helpful to start by learning to set the right temperature for basic foods:

- **Low Heat (200-300°F)** is ideal for foods that require slow cooking or gentle warming, such as soft vegetables, eggs, and seafood.

- **Medium Heat (300-400°F)** suits most general cooking needs, perfect for pancakes, grilled cheese sandwiches, and sautéing vegetables.

- **High Heat (400-500°F)** is necessary for searing meats or stir-frying, providing quick, intense heat to brown surfaces while keeping interiors juicy and tender.

To master these settings, begin by lighting the griddle and setting all burners to medium. Allow the griddle surface to heat uniformly. Once you are familiar with the basic heat settings, experiment by adjusting different burners to create warmer and cooler zones. For instance, one side of the griddle can be set to high for searing steaks, while the other side is kept at a lower temperature for grilling vegetables.

A practical tip for managing griddle temperature is to use the hand test: hold your hand about five inches above the griddle surface. The amount of time you can comfortably keep your hand in that position indicates the heat level—quick discomfort suggests high heat, while a longer duration indicates lower temperatures. This method provides a rough guide until you become more accustomed to the heat settings and their effects on different foods.

Additionally, investing in an infrared thermometer can provide precise readings of surface temperatures, which is especially useful for ensuring consistency when cooking sensitive dishes or following specific recipes that require exact heat settings.

Understanding and controlling the temperature on your Blackstone gas griddle not only ensures delicious, well-cooked meals but also enhances your confidence and enjoyment in griddle cooking. This knowledge lays the foundation for exploring more complex recipes and techniques, as you'll learn to adjust the heat intuitively based on the dish you're preparing.

Tools of the Trade: Essential Utensils for Effective Griddle Cooking

To truly excel in griddle cooking and ensure each meal is a culinary delight, having the right tools is crucial. I've personally tested and selected the following products, which have significantly enhanced my cooking experience. These are tools I use and recommend because they consistently perform well. As an added bonus, using these affiliate links to make your purchases helps support our content at no additional cost to you.

Spatulas: A good set of spatulas can make all the difference on a griddle. I use these because they're sturdy and have a wide surface, perfect for flipping everything from pancakes to burgers with ease. Their durable design means they withstand the heat and activity of griddle cooking flawlessly. Find them here: https://amzn.to/3LPfPqt

Scrapers: Keeping your griddle clean while you cook is key to great flavors and safe food preparation. This scraper is an essential in my toolkit. It's tough on burnt residues but gentle enough not to damage the griddle surface. A clean griddle means better tasting and healthier meals. Find them here: https://amzn.to/3StHyB3

Tongs: When grilling, you need tongs that are both strong and precise. These tongs offer a great grip and long handles, keeping your hands safe from the heat while providing the control you need to manage your food like a pro. Find them here: https://amzn.to/3WlGn7P

Basting Brush: A silicone basting brush like this one is indispensable for applying marinades and sauces. It withstands high temperatures without melting or losing bristles, ensuring your meals are flavored just right every time. Find them here: https://amzn.to/4c9ogaR

Thermometer: To ensure your meats are cooked safely to perfection, an instant-read thermometer is a must-have. It's quick, accurate, and easy to read, which takes the guesswork out of griddle cooking. Find them here: https://amzn.to/3WI09fg

Oil Bottles: These oil bottles with pour spouts make it easy to control the amount of oil you use, ensuring a perfectly oiled griddle every time. They're a simple but essential tool for any griddle chef. Find them here: https://amzn.to/4fngYDm

Griddle Covers: Protecting your griddle from the elements is crucial for its longevity. These griddle covers are durable, fit perfectly, and keep your setup ready for the next cookout. Find them here: https://amzn.to/3LKrEP2

Cleaning Supplies: Good cleaning supplies are the secret to maintaining your griddle in top condition. These supplies make it easy to keep the griddle clean, ensuring it lasts for many seasons and meals. Find them here: https://amzn.to/3LIGvcI

Remember, these are affiliate links, and purchasing through them helps support our content. Thank you for trusting my recommendations and happy griddling!

Maintenance and Cleaning: Daily and Deep-Cleaning Practices to Keep Your Griddle in Prime Condition

Proper maintenance and cleaning of your Blackstone gas griddle are essential for ensuring its longevity and performance. Regular cleaning not only prevents flavor transfer and food contamination but also extends the life of your griddle by preventing rust and degradation. Here's a guide to both daily and deep-cleaning practices that will keep your griddle in top shape.

Daily Cleaning Practices After each use, it's important to clean your griddle to remove food particles and excess grease. Once the griddle has cooled down to a safe temperature but is still warm, scrape off any food residues with a metal scraper. After scraping, wipe the surface with a paper towel to remove loose debris and excess oil. For a more thorough clean, pour some water onto the still-warm griddle and gently scrub using a griddle brush or pad to loosen any stuck-on bits. The water will steam up, making it easier to clean the surface. Finally, dry the griddle thoroughly with a clean cloth or paper towels.

Applying Oil After Cleaning Once the griddle is clean and dry, it's crucial to apply a light coat of cooking oil to the surface. This oiling protects the griddle from moisture and rust, especially if stored outdoors. Use a high smoke point oil such as canola, vegetable, or flaxseed oil, applying it with a cloth or paper towel in a thin, even layer. This routine after each cooking session will help maintain a non-stick surface and prevent rust.

Deep-Cleaning Practices Depending on how frequently you use your griddle, a more thorough deep-cleaning might be necessary every few months or after a particularly heavy usage period. For deep cleaning, heat the griddle to a high temperature to burn off any residual food particles. Once the griddle is hot, turn off the heat and let it cool slightly. Then, using a non-metallic scrub pad and a griddle cleaner or a mixture of hot water and mild dish soap, scrub the entire surface. Rinse the surface well with water and ensure all soap and debris are completely removed.

If you encounter rust, which can happen if the griddle was not properly oiled or left exposed to moisture, you can remove it using a griddle stone or fine-grit sandpaper. Rub the affected areas gently until the rust is gone, clean the surface as per the above steps, and then re-season the griddle by heating it and applying a coat of oil.

Remember, the key to maintaining your griddle in prime condition is regular and proper cleaning. By following these daily and deep-cleaning practices, you ensure that your Blackstone gas griddle remains a reliable and enjoyable tool for your outdoor cooking adventures.

Chapter 3: Griddle Cooking Techniques

Direct vs. Indirect Grilling: When and How to Use Each Method

Understanding the difference between direct and indirect grilling on your Blackstone gas griddle is key to mastering a variety of cooking techniques and achieving optimal results for different types of dishes. Both methods have their specific uses and can be adapted depending on the food you are preparing.

Direct Grilling Direct grilling involves cooking food directly over the heat source. On a Blackstone griddle, this means using the burners to heat the griddle surface and placing food directly above the active burners. This method provides high heat and quick cooking times, making it ideal for searing meats, cooking burgers, frying eggs, or preparing pancakes. The direct heat quickly browns the surface of the food, locking in flavors and creating a delicious crust.

When using direct grilling, it's important to manage the heat carefully to avoid burning the food. The Blackstone's adjustable burners are perfect for this, as you can turn the heat up or down based on the thickness and type of food. For example, thin slices of bacon or quick-cooking shrimp will need a shorter time over medium-high heat, while thicker steak cuts might require high heat initially for searing, then a lower temperature to finish cooking through.

Indirect Grilling Indirect grilling on a griddle is slightly different from how it's traditionally used in closed-lid barbecue grills, but the principle remains the same. It involves cooking food away from the direct heat source, using the ambient heat to cook the food more slowly. On a Blackstone griddle, this can be achieved by turning on one or more burners to high heat and leaving other areas of the griddle at a lower temperature or completely off.

This method is especially useful for cooking larger items like whole chickens, thick roasts, or dense vegetables that need to cook through without burning on the outside. You can start these items over direct heat to get a good sear and then move them to a cooler part of the griddle to finish cooking. This technique is also excellent for foods that need to stay on the griddle for longer periods, such as slow-cooked caramelized onions or a batch of simmering barbecue sauce.

Combining Techniques For many meals, you'll find that a combination of both direct and indirect grilling methods works best. You can sear meats directly over the heat to develop flavor and texture and then move them to a cooler part of the griddle to cook through to the desired doneness. This combination approach allows for greater control over cooking temperatures, helping you to manage different components of your meal simultaneously.

By mastering both direct and indirect grilling techniques on your Blackstone griddle, you expand your cooking versatility significantly. Whether you're whipping up a quick breakfast or hosting a full dinner party, these methods will help you to efficiently and deliciously cook a wide range of dishes.

The Art of Searing: Techniques for Perfect Sear Marks

Searing is a fundamental griddle cooking technique that enhances the flavor and appearance of foods, especially meats. The goal of searing is to create a rich, caramelized crust that locks in moisture and intensifies flavors. On a Blackstone gas griddle, achieving perfect sear marks is both an art and a science, requiring precise heat management and timing.

Preheat the Griddle For optimal searing, your griddle should be preheated to a high temperature. This usually means setting the burners to high and allowing the griddle surface to heat up for at least 10 to 15 minutes. A hot griddle is crucial as it ensures the immediate browning of the surface of the meat, which is essential for a good sear.

Use the Right Oil Choose an oil with a high smoke point to avoid burning and unpleasant flavors. Oils like canola, avocado, or grapeseed oil are ideal for searing because they withstand high temperatures without smoking excessively. Apply a thin layer of oil to the griddle surface just before adding your food; this helps create a non-stick surface and contributes to the formation of even and attractive sear marks.

Avoid Overcrowding Place the items on the griddle with enough space between them to ensure they are not steaming in their own juices. Overcrowding the griddle surface lowers the temperature and prevents the foods from searing correctly. This space also allows for better air circulation, which helps maintain the high surface temperature necessary for searing.

Don't Move the Food Prematurely After placing your meat or vegetables on the griddle, let them cook undisturbed for a few minutes. Moving them too early can prevent the sear marks from forming and may cause the food to stick. Once the food releases easily from the griddle, it's usually a good indicator that it has seared properly and is ready to be flipped.

Control the Cooking Time The duration of searing will depend on the type of food and its thickness. For instance, a steak might need about 3-4 minutes per side to develop perfect sear marks, while thinner items like fish fillets might require less time. Use visual cues and an instant-read thermometer to judge when the food has cooked to your preference.

Finish Cooking if Necessary For thicker cuts of meat, after you've achieved the desired sear marks, you may need to lower the heat or move the food to a cooler part of the griddle to finish cooking internally without burning the exterior. This method ensures that your meat is flavorful and juicy inside with a perfectly seared exterior.

Mastering the art of searing on your Blackstone gas griddle will elevate your cooking, impressing both family and guests with the professional-quality results. By following these techniques, you can enjoy beautifully seared meats and vegetables with minimal effort, making every meal a special occasion.

Layering Flavors: Using Marinades, Rubs, and Sauces

Flavor layering is an essential technique in cooking that enhances the taste and complexity of dishes. On the Blackstone gas griddle, utilizing marinades, rubs, and sauces can elevate simple ingredients into gourmet-level meals. Each method brings distinct flavors and textures to the table, allowing you to craft dishes that are rich in taste and appeal.

Marinades: Marinades are mixtures of acid (like vinegar or citrus juice), oil, and seasonings that tenderize and infuse food with flavor before cooking. They are particularly useful for tougher cuts of meat or firmer vegetables, softening them and adding moisture. When using a marinade on the Blackstone griddle, allow the food to soak in the mixture for several hours or even overnight in the refrigerator to maximize flavor penetration. Before placing the items on the griddle, let them come to room temperature and drain off excess marinade to prevent flare-ups and ensure a good sear.

Rubs: Rubs are blends of spices and seasonings applied directly to the surface of food. They create a crust that adds texture and concentrated flavor. Rubs can be dry or wet (mixed with a small amount of oil or other liquid to form a paste). When using rubs, apply them generously to the surface of the meat or vegetables and let them sit for at least 30 minutes before grilling. This resting period helps the flavors to meld and adhere to the food, ensuring they don't simply fall off during cooking.

Sauces: Sauces can be applied before, during, or after grilling. When used during cooking, they should be applied in the last few minutes to prevent sugars from burning and to allow the sauce to thicken and cling to the food. Barbecue sauce, for example, is perfect for adding a final touch of flavor and achieving a sticky, caramelized finish. Post-cooking applications, like drizzling a balsamic glaze over grilled vegetables or adding a dollop of herb butter to a steak, add a fresh burst of flavor and enhance the dish's visual appeal.

For the best results on the Blackstone griddle:

- Start with a base layer of seasoning before cooking, such as a rub or a light brush of oil mixed with herbs.
- Add marinades to meats and vegetables well in advance to deepen their flavors.
- Finish with a sauce or glaze to complement and enhance the natural tastes of the ingredients.

Using these techniques allows you to build layers of flavor that make each dish complex and satisfying. Experimenting with different combinations of marinades, rubs, and sauces can turn even the simplest ingredients into a feast of flavors on your Blackstone griddle.

Whether you're aiming for a subtle enhancement or a bold taste transformation, these methods will help you achieve delicious results every time.

Chapter 4: Ingredients and Preparations

Choosing the Right Ingredients: Best Meats, Vegetables, and Other Foods for Griddling

Selecting the right ingredients is crucial for achieving the best results on your Blackstone gas griddle. The griddle's high heat and wide cooking surface make it ideal for a variety of foods, from meats and vegetables to seafood and even fruits. Here's a guide to help you choose the best ingredients for griddling, ensuring delicious outcomes every time.

Meats: When it comes to griddling, not all cuts of meat are created equal. High-quality, well-marbled meats such as ribeye steaks, pork chops, and chicken thighs are ideal because they can withstand high temperatures and remain juicy and flavorful. Ground meat for burgers or meatballs should have a higher fat content to prevent drying out during cooking. For more delicate options, thinner cuts like flank steak or skirt steak are excellent as they cook quickly and absorb marinades well, which enhances their flavor on the griddle.

Vegetables: Most vegetables can be cooked on a griddle, but some are particularly well-suited to this cooking method. Denser vegetables like bell peppers, onions, asparagus, and zucchini have a robust structure that holds up well to high heat. Slice them uniformly to ensure even cooking. Mushrooms, corn on the cob, and cherry tomatoes also perform beautifully, developing rich, smoky flavors and attractive grill marks. For a quick and healthy side dish, try griddling sliced sweet potatoes or cauliflower steaks until they're tender and caramelized.

Seafood: Seafood cooks quickly and benefits from the even heat distribution of a griddle. Shrimp, scallops, and firm fish like salmon or tuna are perfect for griddling. They sear nicely and retain a moist interior. When griddling more delicate fish, such as tilapia or cod, use a fish basket or place them on a layer of citrus slices (like lemon or lime) to prevent sticking and add a hint of flavor.

Other Foods: The versatility of the Blackstone griddle extends beyond traditional savory items. For breakfast, try griddling pancakes or French toast, which benefit from the even heat and come out perfectly browned every time. Fruits like pineapple slices, peach halves, or sliced apples can be griddled for a delicious dessert or salad topping, their natural sugars caramelizing beautifully at high temperatures.

Preparation Tips: Proper preparation is key to successful griddling. Marinate or season your ingredients beforehand to enhance their flavors. Make sure meats are at room temperature before they hit the griddle to ensure even cooking. Vegetables should be lightly oiled and seasoned to prevent sticking and to improve taste. Keep seafood portions uniform for consistent cooking, and consider brushing them with a light layer of oil or a glaze to protect their delicate textures.

By choosing the right ingredients and preparing them properly, you can maximize the potential of your Blackstone gas griddle and create a wide array of tasty and visually appealing dishes. Whether you're hosting a barbecue, preparing a family meal, or just experimenting with new recipes, the right choices will lead to better flavors and more enjoyable cooking experiences.

Preparation Tips: Marinating, Cutting, and Portioning for the Griddle

Effective preparation is vital for maximizing the potential of your Blackstone gas griddle. Marinating, cutting, and portioning your ingredients correctly not only enhances the cooking process but also elevates the flavors of your dishes. Here are some essential tips to ensure your ingredients are griddle-ready.

Marinating: Marinating adds depth and complexity to the flavor of foods, and it can also tenderize tougher cuts of meat. To marinate effectively:

- **Choose the right marinade**: For meats, a mixture of acids (like vinegar or citrus juice), oils, and seasonings works best. Vegetables and seafood benefit from lighter marinades, often just involving herbs, spices, and oil.

- **Timing is crucial**: Marinate meats like beef or pork for several hours or even overnight in the refrigerator to allow the flavors to penetrate deeply. Chicken and vegetables can marinate for a few hours, while seafood should only be marinated for up to an hour to prevent the acids from cooking the flesh prematurely.

- **Use resealable bags**: To ensure even coverage and save space in your fridge, use resealable plastic bags for marinating. Make sure to turn the bags occasionally to distribute the marinade evenly.

Cutting: Proper cutting ensures uniform cooking and optimal texture:

- **Uniform thickness**: Cut meats and vegetables to a consistent thickness to promote even cooking. For instance, steaks should be about the same thickness, and vegetable slices should be uniform to ensure they all cook at the same rate.

- **Pre-cut vegetables**: For mixed dishes like stir-fries, pre-cut all vegetables in advance to similar sizes to keep cooking times consistent when they hit the griddle.

- **Meat slicing**: When slicing meat, always cut against the grain. This breaks up the muscle fibers and results in more tender cooked meat.

Portioning: Correct portioning helps in managing cooking space and time efficiently on the griddle:

- **Individual portions**: Portion meats and vegetables into individual servings before cooking. This makes it easier to manage cooking times and turn the ingredients on the griddle.

- **Space management**: When planning your cooking, consider the space each item will need. Don't overcrowd the griddle; leave enough room to easily maneuver and flip the items.

By marinating your ingredients appropriately, cutting them for uniform cooking, and portioning them correctly for the space on your griddle, you can ensure that every meal you prepare is cooked efficiently and tastes fantastic. These preparation steps are simple but crucial for leveraging the full capabilities of your Blackstone gas griddle, allowing you to enjoy the cooking process as much as the delicious results.

Part II: Recipes

Chapter 5: Quick and Easy Griddle Meals

This chapter focuses on convenience without sacrificing flavor, featuring 12 recipes that can be prepared on your Blackstone griddle in 30 minutes or less. These meals are perfect for busy weekday dinners, offering a variety of options to satisfy different tastes and dietary preferences.

Classic Cheeseburgers

Servings: 4
Prep Time: 10 minutes
Cooking Time: 10 minutes
Description: Juicy, flavorful burgers topped with melty cheese, served on toasted buns with your favorite condiments.
Ingredients:

- 1 pound ground beef (80/20)
- 4 slices of cheese (cheddar or American)
- 4 hamburger buns
- Lettuce, tomato, onions, pickles
- Salt and pepper
- Condiments (ketchup, mustard, mayonnaise)

Preparation Steps:
Begin by preheating the griddle to medium-high. Form the ground beef into four patties, slightly larger than the buns, and season both sides with salt and pepper. Place the patties on the hot griddle, cooking for about 5 minutes on each side or until the desired doneness is reached. A minute before the burgers are done, place a slice of cheese on each patty to melt. Meanwhile, toast the hamburger buns on the griddle until golden. Serve the burgers on the toasted buns with lettuce, tomato, onions, pickles, and your preferred condiments.

Vegetable Stir-Fry

Servings: 4
Prep Time: 15 minutes
Cooking Time: 10 minutes
Description: A vibrant and colorful mix of fresh vegetables sautéed on a hot griddle, flavored with soy sauce and sesame oil for a quick and healthy side dish or meal.
Ingredients:

- 1 bell pepper, sliced
- 1 zucchini, sliced

- 1 carrot, julienned
- 1 onion, sliced
- 1 cup broccoli florets
- 2 cloves garlic, minced
- 2 tablespoons soy sauce
- 1 tablespoon sesame oil
- 1 teaspoon fresh ginger, grated
- Salt and pepper to taste
- Optional: sesame seeds for garnish

Preparation Steps:
Start by preheating your Blackstone griddle to medium-high. Prepare all the vegetables by slicing them uniformly to ensure even cooking. Once the griddle is hot, add sesame oil followed by garlic and ginger, sautéing briefly until fragrant. Add the harder vegetables first, such as carrots and broccoli, cooking for a couple of minutes before adding softer vegetables like bell peppers, zucchini, and onions. Stir and toss the vegetables frequently to prevent burning and ensure they cook evenly. Drizzle soy sauce over the vegetables and continue to cook for another 5 minutes or until all vegetables are tender yet crisp. Season with salt and pepper, and garnish with sesame seeds if desired. Serve hot as a side dish or over rice for a fulfilling meal.

Chicken Quesadillas

Servings: 4
Prep Time: 15 minutes
Cooking Time: 10 minutes
Description: Cheesy, crispy quesadillas filled with seasoned chicken, peppers, onions, and a blend of cheeses, grilled to perfection for a quick and satisfying meal.
Ingredients:

- 2 cups cooked chicken, shredded
- 4 large flour tortillas
- 1 cup cheddar cheese, shredded
- 1 cup Monterey Jack cheese, shredded
- 1 bell pepper, thinly sliced
- 1 onion, thinly sliced
- 1 teaspoon chili powder
- 1/2 teaspoon cumin
- Salt and pepper to taste
- Olive oil or butter for cooking

Preparation Steps:
Begin by mixing the shredded chicken with chili powder, cumin, salt, and pepper in a bowl to ensure the chicken is evenly seasoned. Heat the Blackstone griddle over medium heat and lightly brush with olive oil or butter. Place a tortilla on the griddle and on one half of the tortilla, layer a portion of both types of cheese, seasoned chicken, bell pepper, and onion. Fold the other half of the tortilla over the fillings to form a half-moon shape. Cook for about 3 to 5 minutes on each side or until the tortillas are golden brown and the

cheese has melted completely. Repeat with the remaining tortillas. Serve the quesadillas hot, cut into wedges, ideally accompanied by salsa, sour cream, or guacamole for dipping.

Grilled Shrimp Skewers

Servings: 4
Prep Time: 20 minutes (includes marinating time)
Cooking Time: 5 minutes
Description: Succulent shrimp marinated in a zesty lime and garlic mixture, threaded onto skewers, and grilled to perfection for a light and flavorful dish.
Ingredients:

- 1 pound large shrimp, peeled and deveined
- 2 cloves garlic, minced
- Juice of 1 lime
- 2 tablespoons olive oil
- 1 teaspoon paprika
- 1/2 teaspoon chili flakes
- Salt and pepper to taste
- Fresh cilantro, chopped for garnish
- Lime wedges, for serving

Preparation Steps:
Start by preparing the marinade in a mixing bowl by combining the olive oil, lime juice, minced garlic, paprika, chili flakes, salt, and pepper. Add the shrimp to the marinade and toss to coat thoroughly. Allow the shrimp to marinate in the refrigerator for about 15 minutes. While the shrimp marinate, preheat your Blackstone griddle to high heat. Thread the marinated shrimp onto skewers, packing them tightly to ensure even cooking. Place the skewers on the hot griddle and cook for about 2 to 3 minutes on each side, or until the shrimp are opaque and slightly charred. Be careful not to overcook as shrimp cook quickly and can become tough if left too long on the heat. Remove the skewers from the griddle and garnish with chopped cilantro. Serve immediately with lime wedges on the side for an extra burst of citrus flavor.

Steak and Mushrooms

Servings: 4
Prep Time: 10 minutes
Cooking Time: 15 minutes
Description: Tender, juicy steaks paired with savory sautéed mushrooms, cooked together on the griddle for a delicious and hearty meal.
Ingredients:

- 4 steaks (such as ribeye or sirloin), about 1 inch thick
- 2 cups mushrooms, sliced
- 2 tablespoons butter

- 1 tablespoon olive oil
- 2 cloves garlic, minced
- Salt and freshly ground black pepper
- Fresh thyme or rosemary (optional)

Preparation Steps:

Begin by allowing the steaks to come to room temperature, which promotes even cooking. Season both sides of each steak generously with salt and pepper. Heat the Blackstone griddle to a high temperature for searing. Once hot, add the olive oil and steaks to the griddle. Cook the steaks for about 6-7 minutes per side for medium-rare, adjusting the time based on thickness and desired doneness. While the steaks are cooking, add butter to another area of the griddle. Once melted, add the sliced mushrooms and minced garlic, sautéing until the mushrooms are golden and soft, which usually takes about 8-10 minutes. If using, sprinkle some fresh thyme or rosemary over the mushrooms for added flavor. Once the steaks are cooked to your preference, remove them from the griddle and let them rest for a few minutes before serving alongside the sautéed mushrooms. This allows the juices in the steaks to redistribute, ensuring each bite is succulent and flavorful.

Griddled Breakfast Sandwiches

Servings: 4
Prep Time: 10 minutes
Cooking Time: 10 minutes
Description: Hearty and satisfying breakfast sandwiches made with crispy bacon, fried eggs, and melted cheese, all stacked between toasted English muffins.
Ingredients:

- 4 English muffins, split
- 8 slices bacon
- 4 large eggs
- 4 slices cheese (such as cheddar or American)
- Butter for griddling
- Salt and pepper to taste

Preparation Steps:

Start by heating your Blackstone griddle to medium heat. Add the bacon slices to the griddle and cook until crispy, about 3 to 4 minutes per side. Remove the bacon from the griddle and set aside. In the bacon fat remaining on the griddle, crack the eggs, being careful to keep them separate. Season with salt and pepper and cook until the whites are set but the yolks are still runny, or cook longer if you prefer firmer yolks. While the eggs are cooking, butter the cut sides of the English muffins and place them on the griddle to toast until golden brown. To assemble the sandwiches, place a slice of cheese on the bottom half of each muffin, top with two slices of bacon, add the fried egg, and cover with the other half of the muffin. Serve hot for a delicious and energizing start to your day.

Spicy Sausage and Peppers

Servings: 4
Prep Time: 10 minutes
Cooking Time: 15 minutes
Description: A sizzling dish of spicy sausages, sautéed bell peppers, and onions, perfect for a flavorful and filling meal.
Ingredients:

- 4 spicy Italian sausages
- 2 bell peppers, sliced (use a mix of colors for visual appeal)
- 1 large onion, sliced
- 2 tablespoons olive oil
- Salt and pepper to taste
- Optional: crushed red pepper flakes for extra heat

Preparation Steps:
Preheat your Blackstone griddle over medium-high heat. Begin by adding the olive oil to the griddle, then place the sausages on the griddle to start cooking. Turn them occasionally to ensure even cooking and browning on all sides, which should take about 10 minutes. As the sausages cook, add the sliced bell peppers and onions to another part of the griddle. Season the vegetables with salt, pepper, and optional red pepper flakes if you like a spicier dish. Sauté the vegetables until they are soft and slightly charred, about 10 minutes, stirring frequently to promote even cooking and prevent burning. Once the sausages are cooked through and the vegetables are tender, slice the sausages into bite-sized pieces if desired and mix them with the peppers and onions on the griddle for an additional minute to let the flavors meld. Serve hot, perhaps with crusty bread or over a bed of rice for a complete meal.

Turkey and Spinach Wraps

Servings: 4
Prep Time: 10 minutes
Cooking Time: 5 minutes
Description: Light and healthy wraps filled with seasoned turkey, fresh spinach, and a touch of creamy dressing, perfect for a quick lunch or a snack.
Ingredients:

- 1 pound ground turkey
- 4 large flour tortillas
- 2 cups fresh spinach
- 1/2 cup grated carrot
- 1/4 cup diced red onion
- 1 teaspoon garlic powder
- 1 teaspoon onion powder
- Salt and pepper to taste

- 1/4 cup Greek yogurt or mayonnaise
- Optional: avocado slices or shredded cheese

Preparation Steps:
Begin by preheating your Blackstone griddle to medium heat. In a bowl, mix the ground turkey with garlic powder, onion powder, salt, and pepper. Place the seasoned turkey on the griddle and cook, breaking it into smaller pieces with a spatula as it cooks, until it is thoroughly cooked and no longer pink, about 5 minutes. Remove from heat. Lay out the flour tortillas and spread each with a thin layer of Greek yogurt or mayonnaise. Layer the cooked turkey, fresh spinach, grated carrot, and diced red onion onto the tortillas. Add optional ingredients like avocado slices or shredded cheese if desired. Roll up the tortillas tightly to form wraps. If preferred, you can place the wraps back on the griddle for a minute on each side to warm them up and slightly crisp the exterior. Slice each wrap in half and serve immediately for a delicious and nutritious meal.

Salmon and Asparagus

Servings: 4
Prep Time: 10 minutes
Cooking Time: 10 minutes
Description: Elegant yet simple, this dish features perfectly grilled salmon fillets and tender-crisp asparagus, all cooked on the griddle for a meal that's both healthy and delicious.
Ingredients:

- 4 salmon fillets, about 6 ounces each
- 1 bunch asparagus, ends trimmed
- 2 tablespoons olive oil
- 1 lemon, sliced
- Salt and freshly ground black pepper
- Optional: herbs such as dill or parsley for garnish

Preparation Steps:
Start by preheating your Blackstone griddle to medium-high heat. Brush both the salmon fillets and asparagus with olive oil and season generously with salt and pepper. Place the salmon fillets skin-side down on the griddle if they have skin, along with the asparagus spears. Arrange lemon slices around the griddle to add a citrusy aroma and slight tang to the dishes as they cook. Grill the salmon for about 5 minutes on each side or until the flesh flakes easily with a fork. The asparagus will cook in about the same time, turning occasionally, until they are tender and have grill marks. Once cooked, transfer the salmon and asparagus to plates, garnish with fresh herbs if desired, and serve immediately, perhaps with additional lemon wedges for squeezing over the fish. This dish pairs beautifully with a light salad or a side of quinoa for a complete meal.

BBQ Chicken Pizza

Servings: 4
Prep Time: 15 minutes
Cooking Time: 10 minutes
Description: A smoky, savory pizza topped with barbecue chicken, onions, and cheese, cooked directly on the griddle for a crisp crust and bubbly top.
Ingredients:

- 1 pre-made pizza dough or flatbread
- 1 cup cooked chicken, shredded
- 1/2 cup barbecue sauce, plus more for drizzling
- 1/2 red onion, thinly sliced
- 1 cup mozzarella cheese, shredded
- 1/4 cup cilantro, chopped
- Olive oil for brushing

Preparation Steps:
Begin by preheating your Blackstone griddle to medium-high heat. Roll out the pizza dough on a lightly floured surface to your desired thickness. Lightly brush one side of the dough with olive oil and place it oil-side down on the hot griddle. Cook for about 2-3 minutes or until the bottom starts to brown and crisp up. Brush the top side with olive oil, then flip the crust. Quickly spread the barbecue sauce over the cooked side, then top with shredded chicken, sliced red onion, and mozzarella cheese. Close the griddle if it has a lid, or cover the pizza with a large metal bowl or foil to melt the cheese and heat the toppings, about 5-7 minutes. Once the cheese is bubbly and the bottom of the crust is crispy, remove the pizza from the griddle. Sprinkle chopped cilantro over the top, drizzle with a little more barbecue sauce if desired, and cut into slices. Serve hot for a delicious twist on traditional pizza night.

Pork Chops with Apple Slaw

Servings: 4
Prep Time: 15 minutes
Cooking Time: 10 minutes
Description: Succulent pork chops grilled to perfection, accompanied by a fresh and tangy apple slaw, making for a balanced and refreshing meal.
Ingredients:

- 4 bone-in pork chops, about 1 inch thick
- Salt and freshly ground black pepper
- 2 tablespoons olive oil
- 2 medium apples, julienned (such as Granny Smith or Honeycrisp)
- 1/4 cabbage, shredded
- 1 carrot, julienned
- 2 tablespoons mayonnaise

- 1 tablespoon cider vinegar
- 1 teaspoon honey
- Salt and pepper to taste for the slaw

Preparation Steps:
Season the pork chops with salt and pepper. Preheat your Blackstone griddle to medium-high heat and brush it with olive oil. Place the pork chops on the griddle and cook for about 5 minutes on each side, or until they reach an internal temperature of 145°F (63°C), ensuring they are cooked through yet still juicy. While the pork chops are grilling, prepare the apple slaw. In a large mixing bowl, combine the julienned apples, shredded cabbage, and carrot. In a smaller bowl, whisk together the mayonnaise, cider vinegar, honey, and a pinch of salt and pepper to make the dressing. Pour the dressing over the apple slaw and toss well to coat all the ingredients evenly. Allow the pork chops to rest for a few minutes after grilling to let the juices redistribute. Serve the pork chops with a generous helping of the apple slaw on the side, offering a crisp and tangy contrast to the savory chops. This dish pairs wonderfully with a light, crisp white wine or a refreshing apple cider.

Garlic Butter Scallops

Servings: 4
Prep Time: 10 minutes
Cooking Time: 5 minutes
Description: Tender scallops seared in a rich garlic butter sauce, creating a luxurious yet simple dish that's perfect for impressing guests or treating yourself on a special occasion.
Ingredients:

- 1 pound large sea scallops, side muscle removed
- 4 tablespoons butter
- 3 cloves garlic, minced
- Salt and freshly ground black pepper
- Juice of 1 lemon
- Fresh parsley, chopped for garnish

Preparation Steps:
Pat the scallops dry with paper towels to ensure they sear properly. Season them lightly with salt and pepper. Preheat your Blackstone griddle to high heat and add the butter. Once the butter is melted and starting to bubble, add the minced garlic and sauté for about 1 minute until fragrant but not browned. Place the scallops on the griddle, ensuring they are not touching to avoid steaming. Cook the scallops for about 2 minutes on each side, or until they have a golden crust on each side and are just cooked through. Be careful not to overcook as they can become tough. Drizzle lemon juice over the cooked scallops and sprinkle with chopped parsley for added flavor and color. Serve immediately, ideally with a side of light pasta, steamed vegetables, or a fresh salad to complement the richness of the garlic butter sauce.

Chapter 6: Hearty Breakfasts

This chapter brings together 12 delicious breakfast recipes, ranging from traditional favorites to unique twists on morning classics. Whether you're looking for a quick bite or a leisurely brunch, these recipes provide the perfect start to any day, all prepared on your Blackstone griddle.

Classic Pancakes

Servings: 4
Prep Time: 5 minutes
Cooking Time: 10 minutes
Description: Fluffy, golden pancakes served with butter and maple syrup for a timeless breakfast treat.
Ingredients:

- 2 cups all-purpose flour
- 2 tablespoons sugar
- 2 teaspoons baking powder
- 1/2 teaspoon salt
- 2 eggs
- 1 1/2 cups milk
- 4 tablespoons melted butter
- Extra butter for griddling
- Maple syrup for serving

Preparation Steps:
Mix the flour, sugar, baking powder, and salt in a large bowl. In another bowl, whisk together the eggs, milk, and melted butter. Combine the wet and dry ingredients, stirring until just mixed. Preheat the griddle to medium heat and lightly butter it. Pour batter in 1/4 cup portions onto the griddle. Cook until bubbles form on the surface, then flip and cook until golden brown. Serve with butter and syrup.

Crispy Bacon

Servings: 4
Prep Time: 2 minutes
Cooking Time: 8 minutes
Description: Perfectly crispy bacon strips, a must-have side for any hearty breakfast.
Ingredients:

- 1 pound bacon

Preparation Steps:
Preheat your Blackstone griddle to medium-high heat. Place the bacon strips on the

griddle, making sure they are not overlapping. Cook for about 4 minutes on each side, or until the bacon reaches your desired level of crispiness. Use tongs to flip the bacon halfway through the cooking time. Once cooked, transfer the bacon to a plate lined with paper towels to drain the excess grease. Serve immediately, alongside your favorite breakfast dishes.

Cheese Omelets

Servings: 4
Prep Time: 5 minutes
Cooking Time: 10 minutes
Description: Soft and fluffy omelets filled with melted cheese, perfect for a satisfying breakfast.
Ingredients:

- 8 eggs
- 1/4 cup milk
- Salt and freshly ground black pepper
- 1 cup shredded cheese (cheddar, mozzarella, or your favorite)
- 2 tablespoons butter
- Optional: chopped herbs (such as parsley or chives) for garnish

Preparation Steps:
In a large bowl, whisk together the eggs, milk, salt, and pepper until well combined. Preheat the Blackstone griddle to medium heat and add the butter, allowing it to melt and coat the surface. Pour a portion of the egg mixture onto the griddle, spreading it out to form a round omelet. Cook until the edges start to set, then sprinkle a quarter of the shredded cheese over half of the omelet. Carefully fold the omelet in half over the cheese and cook for another minute until the cheese is melted. Repeat with the remaining egg mixture and cheese to make four omelets. Garnish with chopped herbs if desired and serve hot.

Hash Browns

Servings: 4
Prep Time: 10 minutes
Cooking Time: 15 minutes
Description: Golden, crispy hash browns that are a perfect addition to any breakfast.
Ingredients:

- 4 large russet potatoes, peeled and grated
- 1 small onion, grated
- 2 tablespoons butter
- 2 tablespoons olive oil
- Salt and freshly ground black pepper
- Optional: chopped parsley for garnish

Preparation Steps:
Start by rinsing the grated potatoes in cold water to remove excess starch, then drain and pat them dry with a clean kitchen towel. In a large bowl, combine the grated potatoes and onion, then season with salt and pepper. Preheat your Blackstone griddle to medium-high heat and add the butter and olive oil, allowing them to melt and coat the surface. Spread the potato mixture evenly on the griddle in a thin layer. Cook for about 7-8 minutes on each side, pressing down occasionally with a spatula, until the hash browns are golden brown and crispy. Once cooked, remove the hash browns from the griddle and drain on paper towels if needed. Serve hot, garnished with chopped parsley if desired.

Eggs Benedict

Servings: 4
Prep Time: 15 minutes
Cooking Time: 10 minutes
Description: A classic breakfast dish featuring poached eggs and Canadian bacon on English muffins, topped with rich hollandaise sauce.
Ingredients:

- 4 English muffins, split and toasted
- 8 slices Canadian bacon
- 8 eggs
- 1 tablespoon white vinegar
- 3 egg yolks
- 1/2 cup unsalted butter, melted and warm
- 1 tablespoon lemon juice
- Salt and cayenne pepper to taste
- 1 tablespoon water (optional, for consistency adjustment)

Preparation Steps:
Begin by making the hollandaise sauce. In a blender, combine the egg yolks, lemon juice, salt, and cayenne pepper. Blend on high for about 30 seconds, then slowly drizzle in the warm melted butter while continuing to blend until the sauce is thick and creamy. Adjust the consistency with a little water if necessary. Keep the sauce warm. Preheat the Blackstone griddle to medium heat. Cook the Canadian bacon slices on the griddle until they are heated through and slightly browned, about 2-3 minutes per side. Bring a large pot of water to a gentle simmer and add the white vinegar. Crack each egg into a small cup, then gently slide them one at a time into the simmering water. Poach the eggs for about 3-4 minutes, until the whites are set but the yolks are still runny. To assemble, place two halves of the toasted English muffins on each plate. Top each half with a slice of Canadian bacon, a poached egg, and a generous spoonful of hollandaise sauce. Serve immediately, garnished with a pinch of cayenne pepper or a sprinkle of fresh herbs if desired.

French Toast

Servings: 4
Prep Time: 10 minutes
Cooking Time: 10 minutes
Description: Classic French toast made with thick slices of bread soaked in a rich egg mixture, cooked to golden perfection and served with your favorite toppings.
Ingredients:

- 8 slices of thick bread (brioche or challah works well)
- 4 eggs
- 1 cup milk
- 1 teaspoon vanilla extract
- 1 teaspoon ground cinnamon
- 2 tablespoons sugar
- Butter for griddling
- Maple syrup and powdered sugar for serving

Preparation Steps:

In a large bowl, whisk together the eggs, milk, vanilla extract, cinnamon, and sugar until well combined. Preheat your Blackstone griddle to medium heat and add a pat of butter, allowing it to melt and coat the surface. Dip each slice of bread into the egg mixture, ensuring both sides are thoroughly soaked. Place the soaked bread slices onto the griddle and cook for about 3-4 minutes on each side, or until they are golden brown and cooked through. Serve the French toast hot, topped with maple syrup and a dusting of powdered sugar. You can also add fresh fruit, whipped cream, or other favorite toppings for extra indulgence.

Breakfast Burritos

Servings: 4
Prep Time: 15 minutes
Cooking Time: 10 minutes
Description: Hearty and customizable breakfast burritos filled with scrambled eggs, sausage, cheese, and veggies, all wrapped in a warm tortilla.
Ingredients:

- 8 large eggs
- 1/4 cup milk
- Salt and pepper to taste
- 1 tablespoon butter
- 4 large flour tortillas
- 1/2 pound breakfast sausage
- 1 cup shredded cheese (cheddar or Monterey Jack)
- 1 cup diced bell peppers
- 1/2 cup diced onions
- 1/2 cup salsa (optional)

- 1/4 cup chopped cilantro (optional)

Preparation Steps:

In a large bowl, whisk together the eggs, milk, salt, and pepper. Preheat your Blackstone griddle to medium heat. Cook the breakfast sausage on the griddle, breaking it into small pieces with a spatula until fully cooked and browned. Move the sausage to one side of the griddle to keep warm. Add the butter to the griddle, and once melted, pour the egg mixture onto the surface. Scramble the eggs gently until they are just set, then mix in the diced bell peppers and onions. Warm the flour tortillas on the griddle for about 30 seconds on each side until they are soft and pliable. To assemble the burritos, lay out each tortilla and fill with a portion of scrambled eggs, sausage, shredded cheese, and optional salsa and cilantro. Roll up the tortillas tightly, folding in the sides to enclose the filling. Serve the breakfast burritos immediately, or wrap them in foil to keep warm until ready to eat.

Sausage Patties

Servings: 4
Prep Time: 10 minutes
Cooking Time: 10 minutes
Description: Flavorful and juicy sausage patties that are perfect for breakfast sandwiches or as a hearty side to your morning meal.
Ingredients:

- 1 pound ground pork
- 1 teaspoon salt
- 1/2 teaspoon black pepper
- 1 teaspoon dried sage
- 1/2 teaspoon dried thyme
- 1/2 teaspoon dried rosemary, crushed
- 1/2 teaspoon garlic powder
- 1/4 teaspoon crushed red pepper flakes (optional)
- 1 tablespoon maple syrup (optional)

Preparation Steps:

In a large bowl, combine the ground pork with salt, black pepper, dried sage, thyme, rosemary, garlic powder, and crushed red pepper flakes. If you like a hint of sweetness, add the maple syrup. Mix until the seasonings are evenly distributed throughout the meat. Form the mixture into 8 equal-sized patties. Preheat your Blackstone griddle to medium heat. Once hot, place the sausage patties on the griddle and cook for about 4-5 minutes on each side, or until they are browned and cooked through to an internal temperature of 160°F (71°C). Serve the sausage patties hot, as part of a breakfast sandwich, alongside eggs, or with your favorite breakfast sides.

Grilled Tomatoes

Servings: 4
Prep Time: 5 minutes
Cooking Time: 5 minutes
Description: Juicy and flavorful grilled tomatoes that make a perfect side dish or addition to any breakfast plate.
Ingredients:

- 4 large tomatoes, halved
- 2 tablespoons olive oil
- Salt and freshly ground black pepper
- 1 teaspoon dried oregano or basil
- Optional: grated Parmesan cheese or fresh herbs for garnish

Preparation Steps:
Preheat your Blackstone griddle to medium-high heat. Brush the cut sides of the tomato halves with olive oil and season with salt, pepper, and dried oregano or basil. Place the tomatoes cut side down on the griddle and cook for about 3-4 minutes, until they are slightly charred and softened. Carefully flip the tomatoes and cook for an additional 1-2 minutes on the other side. If desired, sprinkle grated Parmesan cheese over the top during the last minute of cooking. Remove the tomatoes from the griddle and garnish with fresh herbs if using. Serve hot as a side dish or as a tasty addition to your breakfast.

Avocado Toast

Servings: 4
Prep Time: 10 minutes
Cooking Time: 5 minutes
Description: A simple yet delicious breakfast option featuring creamy avocado spread on toasted bread, topped with a variety of optional garnishes for added flavor and texture.
Ingredients:

- 4 slices of your favorite bread
- 2 ripe avocados
- 1 tablespoon lemon juice
- Salt and freshly ground black pepper
- Optional toppings: cherry tomatoes, red pepper flakes, poached eggs, microgreens, feta cheese, olive oil drizzle

Preparation Steps:
Preheat your Blackstone griddle to medium heat. Place the slices of bread on the griddle and toast them for about 2-3 minutes on each side, or until they are golden brown and crispy. While the bread is toasting, cut the avocados in half, remove the pits, and scoop the flesh into a bowl. Add the lemon juice, salt, and pepper to the avocados and mash them together until you reach your desired consistency. Once the bread is toasted, spread

a generous amount of the mashed avocado mixture onto each slice. Top with any of the optional garnishes you prefer, such as sliced cherry tomatoes, a sprinkle of red pepper flakes, a poached egg, microgreens, crumbled feta cheese, or a drizzle of olive oil. Serve immediately for a fresh and satisfying breakfast.

Blueberry Muffins

Servings: 12 muffins
Prep Time: 15 minutes
Cooking Time: 20 minutes
Description: Deliciously moist blueberry muffins with a golden crust, perfect for breakfast or a sweet snack.
Ingredients:

- 1 1/2 cups all-purpose flour
- 3/4 cup sugar
- 1/2 teaspoon salt
- 2 teaspoons baking powder
- 1/3 cup vegetable oil
- 1 egg
- 1/3 cup milk
- 1 teaspoon vanilla extract
- 1 cup fresh or frozen blueberries
- Optional: coarse sugar for topping

Preparation Steps:
Preheat your oven to 400°F (200°C) and line a muffin tin with paper liners. In a large bowl, combine the flour, sugar, salt, and baking powder. In a separate bowl, whisk together the vegetable oil, egg, milk, and vanilla extract. Pour the wet ingredients into the dry ingredients and stir until just combined. Gently fold in the blueberries. Divide the batter evenly among the muffin cups, filling each about 2/3 full. If desired, sprinkle the tops with coarse sugar for a crunchy finish. Bake for 20-25 minutes, or until a toothpick inserted into the center of a muffin comes out clean. Let the muffins cool in the pan for a few minutes before transferring them to a wire rack to cool completely. Enjoy your homemade blueberry muffins warm or at room temperature.

Spinach and Feta Scramble

Servings: 4
Prep Time: 5 minutes
Cooking Time: 10 minutes
Description: A healthy and flavorful scramble made with fresh spinach and tangy feta cheese, perfect for a nutritious breakfast.
Ingredients:

- 8 large eggs

- 1/4 cup milk
- Salt and freshly ground black pepper
- 1 tablespoon olive oil
- 4 cups fresh spinach, roughly chopped
- 1/2 cup crumbled feta cheese
- Optional: diced tomatoes or red onions for extra flavor

Preparation Steps:

In a large bowl, whisk together the eggs, milk, salt, and pepper until well combined. Preheat your Blackstone griddle to medium heat and add the olive oil. Once the oil is hot, add the chopped spinach and sauté for about 1-2 minutes until wilted. Pour the egg mixture over the spinach, allowing it to spread out on the griddle. Gently stir the eggs as they cook, ensuring they scramble evenly and incorporate the spinach. When the eggs are nearly set but still slightly runny, sprinkle the crumbled feta cheese over the top. Continue to cook for another minute until the eggs are fully set and the cheese is warmed. Remove from the griddle and serve immediately, optionally topped with diced tomatoes or red onions for added flavor and color.

Chapter 7: Lunch on the Griddle

This chapter features 12 delicious and varied lunch recipes that you can prepare on your Blackstone griddle, ranging from classic burgers and hearty sandwiches to fresh salads and flavorful seafood.

Grilled Chicken Sandwiches

Servings: 4
Prep Time: 15 minutes
Cooking Time: 10 minutes
Description: Tender and juicy grilled chicken breasts served on toasted buns with fresh lettuce, tomato, and a tangy sauce, making for a perfect lunch option.
Ingredients:

- 4 boneless, skinless chicken breasts
- 2 tablespoons olive oil
- 1 teaspoon garlic powder
- 1 teaspoon onion powder
- Salt and freshly ground black pepper
- 4 sandwich buns
- Lettuce leaves
- Sliced tomatoes
- 1/2 cup mayonnaise
- 1 tablespoon Dijon mustard
- 1 teaspoon lemon juice
- Optional: sliced red onions, pickles

Preparation Steps:
Begin by preheating your Blackstone griddle to medium-high heat. In a bowl, mix the olive oil, garlic powder, onion powder, salt, and pepper. Brush the chicken breasts with the seasoned oil mixture, ensuring they are well coated. Place the chicken breasts on the hot griddle and cook for about 5-6 minutes on each side, or until the internal temperature reaches 165°F (74°C) and the chicken is cooked through. While the chicken is cooking, lightly toast the sandwich buns on the griddle until golden brown. In a small bowl, combine the mayonnaise, Dijon mustard, and lemon juice to create a tangy sauce. Once the chicken is cooked, assemble the sandwiches by spreading the sauce on the toasted buns, then adding lettuce, tomato slices, and the grilled chicken breasts. Add optional toppings like sliced red onions or pickles if desired. Serve the grilled chicken sandwiches immediately for a delicious and satisfying lunch.

Steak Fajitas

Servings: 4
Prep Time: 15 minutes

Cooking Time: 10 minutes
Description: Juicy strips of marinated steak cooked with vibrant bell peppers and onions, served in warm tortillas with your favorite toppings.
Ingredients:

- 1 pound flank steak or skirt steak
- 2 tablespoons olive oil
- 1 tablespoon lime juice
- 1 teaspoon chili powder
- 1 teaspoon cumin
- 1 teaspoon garlic powder
- Salt and freshly ground black pepper
- 2 bell peppers (any color), sliced
- 1 large onion, sliced
- 8 flour tortillas
- Optional toppings: sour cream, guacamole, salsa, shredded cheese, chopped cilantro

Preparation Steps:

Begin by preparing the steak marinade. In a bowl, combine the olive oil, lime juice, chili powder, cumin, garlic powder, salt, and pepper. Place the steak in a resealable plastic bag or shallow dish, pour the marinade over it, and let it marinate for at least 30 minutes, preferably up to 2 hours in the refrigerator. Preheat your Blackstone griddle to medium-high heat. Remove the steak from the marinade and let any excess drip off. Place the steak on the hot griddle and cook for about 4-5 minutes on each side, or until it reaches your desired level of doneness. Remove the steak from the griddle and let it rest for a few minutes before slicing it against the grain into thin strips. While the steak rests, add the sliced bell peppers and onions to the griddle. Cook the vegetables for about 5 minutes, stirring occasionally, until they are tender and slightly charred. Warm the flour tortillas on the griddle for about 30 seconds on each side. To assemble the fajitas, place some steak strips and cooked vegetables on each tortilla. Add your favorite toppings, such as sour cream, guacamole, salsa, shredded cheese, and chopped cilantro. Serve the steak fajitas immediately for a flavorful and satisfying lunch.

Shrimp Tacos

Servings: 4
Prep Time: 15 minutes
Cooking Time: 5 minutes
Description: Flavorful shrimp seasoned and cooked to perfection, served in warm tortillas with fresh toppings for a delightful and quick lunch.
Ingredients:

- 1 pound large shrimp, peeled and deveined
- 2 tablespoons olive oil
- 1 teaspoon chili powder
- 1/2 teaspoon cumin

- 1/2 teaspoon paprika
- 1/4 teaspoon garlic powder
- Salt and freshly ground black pepper
- 8 small corn or flour tortillas
- 1 cup shredded cabbage
- 1/4 cup chopped red onion
- 1/4 cup chopped fresh cilantro
- 1 lime, cut into wedges
- Optional toppings: avocado slices, sour cream, salsa, hot sauce

Preparation Steps:

Start by preheating your Blackstone griddle to medium-high heat. In a bowl, toss the shrimp with olive oil, chili powder, cumin, paprika, garlic powder, salt, and pepper until well coated. Place the shrimp on the hot griddle and cook for about 2-3 minutes on each side, or until the shrimp are pink and opaque. While the shrimp are cooking, warm the tortillas on the griddle for about 30 seconds on each side. To assemble the tacos, place a few shrimp on each tortilla. Top with shredded cabbage, chopped red onion, and fresh cilantro. Squeeze lime juice over the top and add any optional toppings like avocado slices, sour cream, salsa, or hot sauce. Serve the shrimp tacos immediately for a fresh and delicious lunch.

Vegetarian Panini

Servings: 4
Prep Time: 10 minutes
Cooking Time: 10 minutes
Description: A hearty and flavorful panini filled with grilled vegetables, melted cheese, and fresh pesto, perfect for a satisfying lunch.
Ingredients:

- 1 zucchini, sliced
- 1 red bell pepper, sliced
- 1 yellow bell pepper, sliced
- 1 red onion, sliced
- 4 tablespoons olive oil
- Salt and freshly ground black pepper
- 8 slices of ciabatta or sourdough bread
- 1 cup shredded mozzarella or provolone cheese
- 1/2 cup pesto sauce
- Optional: fresh spinach leaves, sliced tomatoes

Preparation Steps:

Begin by preheating your Blackstone griddle to medium-high heat. In a bowl, toss the zucchini, bell peppers, and red onion with olive oil, salt, and pepper until well coated. Place the vegetables on the griddle and cook for about 5-7 minutes, turning occasionally, until they are tender and slightly charred. Remove the vegetables from the griddle and set aside. To assemble the paninis, spread a layer of pesto sauce on one side of each slice of bread. On four of the slices, layer the grilled vegetables, shredded cheese, and optional fresh spinach leaves or sliced tomatoes. Top with the remaining bread slices, pesto side down. Brush the outside of each sandwich with a little olive oil. Place the assembled sandwiches on the griddle and press them down with a heavy spatula or a grill press. Cook for about 3-4 minutes on each side, or until the bread is golden brown and the cheese is melted. Serve the vegetarian paninis hot, cut in half, for a delicious and wholesome lunch.

Turkey Club Sandwiches

Servings: 4
Prep Time: 10 minutes
Cooking Time: 10 minutes
Description: A classic triple-decker sandwich featuring layers of turkey, bacon, lettuce, tomato, and mayonnaise, perfect for a hearty lunch.
Ingredients:

- 12 slices of bread (white or whole wheat)
- 1 pound cooked turkey breast, thinly sliced
- 8 slices bacon, cooked until crispy
- 1 large tomato, sliced
- 4 leaves of lettuce
- 1/2 cup mayonnaise
- Salt and freshly ground black pepper
- Butter for toasting

Preparation Steps:
Start by preheating your Blackstone griddle to medium heat. Lightly butter one side of each slice of bread. Place the bread slices, butter side down, on the griddle and toast until golden brown, about 2-3 minutes per side. Remove the toasted bread from the griddle. To assemble each sandwich, spread a thin layer of mayonnaise on one side of three slices of toasted bread. On the first slice, layer turkey, followed by a second slice of bread, mayonnaise side up. Add lettuce, tomato slices, bacon, and a pinch of salt and pepper. Top with the third slice of bread, mayonnaise side down. Secure the sandwich with toothpicks and cut it into quarters. Serve the turkey club sandwiches with your favorite side, such as chips, a pickle, or a small salad, for a complete and satisfying lunch.

Grilled Caesar Salad

Servings: 4
Prep Time: 10 minutes
Cooking Time: 5 minutes
Description: A unique twist on the classic Caesar salad, featuring grilled romaine hearts and topped with Caesar dressing, Parmesan cheese, and croutons.
Ingredients:

- 2 romaine hearts, halved lengthwise

- 2 tablespoons olive oil
- Salt and freshly ground black pepper
- 1/2 cup Caesar dressing
- 1/4 cup grated Parmesan cheese
- 1 cup croutons
- Optional: lemon wedges for serving

Preparation Steps:

Preheat your Blackstone griddle to medium-high heat. Brush the cut sides of the romaine hearts with olive oil and season with salt and pepper. Place the romaine hearts cut side down on the griddle and cook for about 2-3 minutes, until they are lightly charred and wilted. Remove the romaine from the griddle and transfer to a serving platter. Drizzle the grilled romaine with Caesar dressing and sprinkle with grated Parmesan cheese. Top with croutons and serve immediately, with optional lemon wedges on the side for an extra burst of flavor. This grilled Caesar salad makes for a refreshing and unique lunch option.

Fish and Chips

Servings: 4
Prep Time: 15 minutes
Cooking Time: 20 minutes
Description: A classic British dish featuring crispy battered fish and golden fries, perfect for a satisfying lunch.
Ingredients:

- 4 white fish fillets (such as cod or haddock)
- 1 cup all-purpose flour
- 1 teaspoon baking powder
- 1 teaspoon salt
- 1/2 teaspoon black pepper
- 1 cup cold sparkling water
- 4 large russet potatoes, cut into fries
- Oil for frying
- Optional: tartar sauce, lemon wedges, and malt vinegar for serving

Preparation Steps:

Begin by preheating your Blackstone griddle to medium-high heat and adding enough oil for shallow frying. In a large bowl, whisk together the flour, baking powder, salt, and pepper. Gradually add the cold sparkling water to the dry ingredients, whisking until you have a smooth batter. Pat the fish fillets dry with paper towels and lightly coat them with a little extra flour, shaking off any excess. Dip each fillet into the batter, ensuring they are well coated. Carefully place the battered fish onto the hot griddle and fry for about 3-4 minutes on each side, or until golden brown and crispy. Transfer the cooked fish to a plate lined with paper towels to drain any excess oil.

While the fish is frying, add the cut potatoes to the griddle in a separate section or use a separate pan. Cook the fries in the hot oil for about 5-7 minutes, turning occasionally until they are golden and crispy. Remove the fries from the oil and drain on paper towels. Season with salt while still hot.

Serve the fish and chips immediately with optional tartar sauce, lemon wedges, and malt vinegar. Enjoy this delicious and comforting dish for lunch.

Philly Cheesesteak

Servings: 4
Prep Time: 10 minutes
Cooking Time: 10 minutes
Description: A classic Philadelphia sandwich featuring thinly sliced beef, sautéed onions and bell peppers, and melted cheese, all served on a toasted hoagie roll.
Ingredients:

- 1 pound ribeye steak, thinly sliced
- 1 large onion, thinly sliced
- 1 green bell pepper, thinly sliced
- 4 hoagie rolls
- 8 slices provolone cheese
- 2 tablespoons olive oil
- Salt and freshly ground black pepper
- Optional: mayonnaise, hot sauce

Preparation Steps:
Preheat your Blackstone griddle to medium-high heat. Add 1 tablespoon of olive oil to the griddle and sauté the sliced onions and bell peppers until they are soft and slightly caramelized, about 5 minutes. Push the vegetables to the side of the griddle to keep warm. Add the remaining tablespoon of olive oil to the griddle, then add the thinly sliced ribeye steak. Season with salt and pepper, and cook for about 2-3 minutes, or until the beef is browned and cooked through. Mix the cooked onions and bell peppers with the beef on the griddle. Divide the mixture into four equal portions and place provolone cheese slices over each portion, allowing the cheese to melt. While the cheese is melting, slice the hoagie rolls and toast them on the griddle until golden brown.

To assemble the sandwiches, spread a thin layer of mayonnaise on the inside of each hoagie roll if desired. Use a spatula to lift each portion of the steak, onion, and pepper mixture and place it onto the toasted hoagie rolls. Serve the Philly cheesesteaks hot, with optional hot sauce on the side. Enjoy this hearty and flavorful sandwich for a satisfying lunch.

Salmon Burgers

Servings: 4
Prep Time: 15 minutes

Cooking Time: 10 minutes
Description: Delicious and healthy salmon patties served on toasted buns with fresh toppings and a tangy sauce, perfect for a light and satisfying lunch.
Ingredients:

- 1 1/2 pounds fresh salmon, skin removed and finely chopped
- 1/4 cup breadcrumbs
- 1 egg, lightly beaten
- 2 green onions, finely chopped
- 2 tablespoons fresh dill, chopped
- 1 tablespoon Dijon mustard
- Salt and freshly ground black pepper
- 2 tablespoons olive oil
- 4 hamburger buns
- Lettuce leaves
- Sliced tomatoes
- 1/4 cup mayonnaise
- 1 tablespoon lemon juice
- 1 teaspoon capers, finely chopped (optional)

Preparation Steps:
In a large bowl, combine the chopped salmon, breadcrumbs, beaten egg, green onions, dill, Dijon mustard, salt, and pepper. Mix well until the ingredients are evenly distributed. Form the mixture into four equal patties, making sure they hold together well. Preheat your Blackstone griddle to medium-high heat and add the olive oil. Once the oil is hot, place the salmon patties on the griddle and cook for about 4-5 minutes on each side, or until they are golden brown and cooked through. While the patties are cooking, toast the hamburger buns on the griddle until they are golden and crispy.

In a small bowl, mix together the mayonnaise, lemon juice, and capers (if using) to create a tangy sauce. To assemble the salmon burgers, spread a generous amount of the sauce on the bottom half of each toasted bun. Add a lettuce leaf, a slice of tomato, and a salmon patty. Top with the other half of the bun and serve immediately. Enjoy these flavorful and healthy salmon burgers for a delicious lunch.

Pesto Chicken Wraps

Servings: 4
Prep Time: 15 minutes
Cooking Time: 10 minutes
Description: Fresh and flavorful wraps filled with grilled chicken, homemade pesto, and crisp vegetables, perfect for a healthy and delicious lunch.
Ingredients:

- 1 pound boneless, skinless chicken breasts
- Salt and freshly ground black pepper
- 2 tablespoons olive oil
- 4 large flour tortillas

- 1 cup fresh basil pesto (store-bought or homemade)
- 1 cup cherry tomatoes, halved
- 1 cup fresh spinach leaves
- 1/2 cup shredded mozzarella cheese
- Optional: sliced avocado, red onion

Preparation Steps:

Begin by preheating your Blackstone griddle to medium-high heat. Season the chicken breasts with salt and pepper on both sides. Add the olive oil to the griddle and place the chicken breasts on it. Cook the chicken for about 5-6 minutes on each side, or until the internal temperature reaches 165°F (74°C) and the chicken is cooked through. Remove the chicken from the griddle and let it rest for a few minutes before slicing it into thin strips.

While the chicken is resting, warm the flour tortillas on the griddle for about 30 seconds on each side until they are soft and pliable. To assemble the wraps, spread a generous layer of basil pesto on each tortilla. Add a handful of fresh spinach leaves, a few cherry tomato halves, and some shredded mozzarella cheese. Place the sliced chicken on top and add any optional ingredients like sliced avocado or red onion. Roll up the tortillas tightly to form wraps, folding in the sides as you go to enclose the filling. Cut the wraps in half and serve immediately. Enjoy these fresh and tasty pesto chicken wraps for a nutritious and satisfying lunch.

Grilled Portobello Mushrooms

Servings: 4
Prep Time: 10 minutes
Cooking Time: 10 minutes
Description: Savory and meaty portobello mushrooms grilled to perfection, served as a main dish or a hearty addition to salads and sandwiches.
Ingredients:

- 4 large portobello mushrooms
- 3 tablespoons olive oil
- 2 tablespoons balsamic vinegar
- 2 cloves garlic, minced
- Salt and freshly ground black pepper
- 4 slices provolone cheese (optional)
- Fresh parsley, chopped for garnish (optional)

Preparation Steps:

Start by cleaning the portobello mushrooms with a damp cloth to remove any dirt. Remove the stems and gently scrape out the gills using a spoon. In a small bowl, whisk together the olive oil, balsamic vinegar, minced garlic, salt, and pepper. Brush the mixture evenly over both sides of the mushrooms. Preheat your Blackstone griddle to medium-high heat. Place the mushrooms on the griddle, gill side up, and cook for about 5 minutes. Flip the mushrooms and cook for another 5 minutes, or until they are tender and have a nice char. If using provolone cheese, place a slice on each mushroom during the last minute of cooking, allowing it to melt.

Remove the mushrooms from the griddle and garnish with chopped fresh parsley if desired. Serve the grilled portobello mushrooms as a main dish, or use them as a flavorful addition to salads, sandwiches, or wraps. Enjoy this hearty and delicious meal that's perfect for both vegetarians and meat-lovers alike.

Queso Fundido with Chorizo

Servings: 4
Prep Time: 10 minutes
Cooking Time: 10 minutes
Description: A rich and savory melted cheese dip mixed with spicy chorizo, perfect for dipping with tortilla chips or warm tortillas.
Ingredients:

- 1/2 pound Mexican chorizo, casing removed
- 2 cups shredded Monterey Jack cheese
- 1 cup shredded Oaxaca or mozzarella cheese
- 1/4 cup diced onion
- 2 cloves garlic, minced
- 1 jalapeño, diced (optional)
- Fresh cilantro, chopped for garnish
- Tortilla chips or warm tortillas for serving

Preparation Steps:
Begin by preheating your Blackstone griddle to medium-high heat. Add the chorizo to the griddle and cook, breaking it up with a spatula, until it is browned and fully cooked. Remove the chorizo from the griddle and set aside, leaving some of the rendered fat on the griddle. Add the diced onion and minced garlic to the griddle and sauté for about 2-3 minutes, or until the onion is soft and translucent. If using, add the diced jalapeño and cook for another minute.

Mix the cooked chorizo back in with the onions, garlic, and jalapeño. Evenly spread the chorizo mixture on the griddle, then sprinkle the shredded Monterey Jack and Oaxaca (or mozzarella) cheeses evenly over the top. Allow the cheese to melt, stirring occasionally to mix the chorizo and cheese together, until it is fully melted and bubbly, about 3-5 minutes. Once the cheese is melted and everything is well combined, remove from the griddle and transfer to a serving dish. Garnish with chopped fresh cilantro. Serve the queso fundido hot with tortilla chips or warm tortillas for dipping. Enjoy this delicious and indulgent appetizer or snack that's perfect for sharing.

Chapter 8: Dinner Feasts

This chapter features 12 gourmet recipes perfect for family dinners and special occasions, including steaks, grilled pizzas, and full platters.

Ribeye Steaks with Garlic Herb Butter

Servings: 4
Prep Time: 15 minutes
Cooking Time: 10 minutes
Description: Juicy and flavorful ribeye steaks topped with a rich garlic herb butter, perfect for a special family dinner or celebration.
Ingredients:

- 4 ribeye steaks, about 1 inch thick
- Salt and freshly ground black pepper
- 2 tablespoons olive oil
- 1/2 cup unsalted butter, softened
- 2 cloves garlic, minced
- 2 tablespoons fresh parsley, chopped
- 1 tablespoon fresh rosemary, chopped
- 1 tablespoon fresh thyme, chopped

Preparation Steps:
Start by preheating your Blackstone griddle to high heat. Season the ribeye steaks generously with salt and freshly ground black pepper on both sides. Drizzle the steaks with olive oil and rub it in to ensure an even coating. Place the steaks on the hot griddle and cook for about 4-5 minutes per side for medium-rare, or adjust the cooking time to reach your desired level of doneness.

While the steaks are cooking, prepare the garlic herb butter. In a small bowl, mix the softened butter with the minced garlic, chopped parsley, rosemary, and thyme until well combined. Once the steaks are done, remove them from the griddle and let them rest for a few minutes to allow the juices to redistribute. Top each steak with a generous dollop of garlic herb butter while they are resting, allowing the butter to melt and enhance the flavor of the steaks.

Serve the ribeye steaks hot, with your favorite side dishes such as mashed potatoes, grilled vegetables, or a fresh salad. Enjoy this gourmet dish that is sure to impress your family and guests.

Grilled Margherita Pizza

Servings: 4
Prep Time: 15 minutes
Cooking Time: 10 minutes
Description: A classic Margherita pizza with a crispy grilled crust, fresh tomatoes, mozzarella, and basil, perfect for a gourmet family dinner.
Ingredients:

- 1 pre-made pizza dough
- 2 tablespoons olive oil
- 2 cloves garlic, minced
- 2 cups fresh tomatoes, sliced
- 1 cup fresh mozzarella, sliced
- Fresh basil leaves
- Salt and freshly ground black pepper
- Balsamic glaze (optional)

Preparation Steps:
Preheat your Blackstone griddle to medium-high heat. Roll out the pizza dough on a floured surface to your desired thickness. Brush one side of the dough with olive oil and place it oil-side down on the griddle. Cook for about 2-3 minutes until the bottom is crispy. Brush the top side with olive oil, then flip the dough. Immediately spread the minced garlic over the dough, then layer with sliced tomatoes and mozzarella. Close the griddle lid or cover the pizza with a large metal bowl to melt the cheese. Cook for another 5-7 minutes until the cheese is bubbly and the crust is golden brown. Remove from the griddle, top with fresh basil leaves, and season with salt and pepper. Drizzle with balsamic glaze if desired. Serve hot.

Surf and Turf Platter

Servings: 4
Prep Time: 20 minutes
Cooking Time: 15 minutes
Description: A luxurious platter featuring juicy steaks and succulent shrimp, ideal for a special family dinner.
Ingredients:

- 4 small filet mignon steaks
- 1 pound large shrimp, peeled and deveined
- 4 tablespoons olive oil, divided
- Salt and freshly ground black pepper
- 2 tablespoons unsalted butter
- 2 cloves garlic, minced
- 1 tablespoon fresh parsley, chopped
- Lemon wedges for serving

Preparation Steps:

Preheat your Blackstone griddle to high heat. Season the filet mignon steaks with salt and pepper. Drizzle 2 tablespoons of olive oil on the griddle and add the steaks. Cook for about 4-5 minutes per side for medium-rare, or adjust the time for your desired doneness. Remove the steaks and let them rest. Drizzle the remaining olive oil on the griddle, then add the shrimp. Cook for 2-3 minutes per side until pink and opaque. In a small saucepan, melt the butter and add the minced garlic, cooking until fragrant. Drizzle the garlic butter over the shrimp. Sprinkle with fresh parsley and serve with lemon wedges. Arrange the steaks and shrimp on a platter and serve immediately.

Stuffed Bell Peppers

Servings: 4
Prep Time: 20 minutes
Cooking Time: 30 minutes
Description: Colorful bell peppers stuffed with a flavorful mixture of ground beef, rice, and vegetables, topped with melted cheese.
Ingredients:

- 4 large bell peppers
- 1 pound ground beef
- 1 cup cooked rice
- 1 small onion, diced
- 1 cup diced tomatoes
- 1 cup shredded cheese (cheddar or mozzarella)
- 2 cloves garlic, minced
- 1 tablespoon olive oil
- Salt and freshly ground black pepper
- Fresh parsley, chopped for garnish

Preparation Steps:

Preheat your Blackstone griddle to medium heat. Cut the tops off the bell peppers and remove the seeds. In a skillet, heat olive oil over medium heat. Add the diced onion and garlic, sautéing until soft. Add the ground beef, cooking until browned. Stir in the cooked rice and diced tomatoes, and season with salt and pepper. Stuff the bell peppers with the beef mixture. Place the stuffed peppers on the griddle and cover with a metal bowl. Cook for about 25-30 minutes until the peppers are tender. In the last 5 minutes, sprinkle the cheese over the tops of the peppers and let it melt. Garnish with fresh parsley and serve hot.

BBQ Ribs

Servings: 4
Prep Time: 20 minutes
Cooking Time: 2 hours
Description: Tender, fall-off-the-bone ribs slow-cooked and basted with a tangy

barbecue sauce, perfect for a family feast.

Ingredients:

- 2 racks baby back ribs
- 1 cup barbecue sauce
- 1/4 cup brown sugar
- 2 tablespoons paprika
- 1 tablespoon garlic powder
- 1 tablespoon onion powder
- Salt and freshly ground black pepper
- 2 tablespoons olive oil

Preparation Steps:

Preheat your Blackstone griddle to low heat. In a small bowl, mix the brown sugar, paprika, garlic powder, onion powder, salt, and pepper. Rub the spice mixture all over the ribs. Drizzle olive oil on the griddle and place the ribs on it, bone-side down. Cover the ribs with foil and cook for about 1.5 to 2 hours, turning occasionally, until the meat is tender. Brush the ribs with barbecue sauce during the last 30 minutes of cooking, allowing the sauce to caramelize. Remove the ribs from the griddle and let them rest for a few minutes before slicing. Serve with extra barbecue sauce on the side.

Mediterranean Grilled Lamb Chops

Servings: 4
Prep Time: 15 minutes
Cooking Time: 10 minutes
Description: Flavorful and tender lamb chops marinated with Mediterranean herbs and spices, grilled to perfection.
Ingredients:

- 8 lamb chops
- 1/4 cup olive oil
- 3 cloves garlic, minced
- 2 tablespoons fresh rosemary, chopped
- 1 tablespoon fresh thyme, chopped
- Juice of 1 lemon
- Salt and freshly ground black pepper
- Optional: tzatziki sauce for serving

Preparation Steps:

In a bowl, combine olive oil, garlic, rosemary, thyme, lemon juice, salt, and pepper. Coat the lamb chops with the marinade and let them sit for at least 30 minutes. Preheat your Blackstone griddle to medium-high heat. Grill the lamb chops for about 4-5 minutes on each side for medium-rare, adjusting the time for your preferred doneness. Let the chops rest for a few minutes before serving. Serve with tzatziki sauce if desired.

Chicken Alfredo Pasta

Servings: 4
Prep Time: 15 minutes
Cooking Time: 20 minutes
Description: Creamy and delicious pasta with grilled chicken, tossed in a rich Alfredo sauce.
Ingredients:

- 1 pound fettuccine pasta
- 2 boneless, skinless chicken breasts
- 2 tablespoons olive oil
- Salt and freshly ground black pepper
- 2 cups heavy cream
- 1 cup grated Parmesan cheese
- 3 cloves garlic, minced
- 2 tablespoons butter
- Fresh parsley, chopped for garnish

Preparation Steps:

Cook the fettuccine according to package instructions. Preheat your Blackstone griddle to medium heat. Season the chicken breasts with salt and pepper, and grill for about 6-7 minutes on each side until cooked through. Remove from heat and slice into strips. In a pan over medium heat, melt the butter and sauté the garlic until fragrant. Add the heavy cream and bring to a simmer. Stir in the Parmesan cheese until the sauce thickens. Toss the cooked pasta and grilled chicken in the Alfredo sauce. Garnish with chopped parsley and serve immediately.

Cedar Plank Salmon

Servings: 4
Prep Time: 10 minutes
Cooking Time: 20 minutes
Description: Delicious salmon fillets grilled on cedar planks, imparting a subtle smoky flavor.
Ingredients:

- 4 salmon fillets
- 2 cedar planks, soaked in water for at least 1 hour
- 1/4 cup olive oil
- 2 tablespoons lemon juice
- 2 cloves garlic, minced
- Salt and freshly ground black pepper
- Fresh dill, chopped for garnish

Preparation Steps:

Preheat your Blackstone griddle to medium-high heat. In a small bowl, combine olive oil, lemon juice, garlic, salt, and pepper. Place the salmon fillets on the cedar planks and brush with the olive oil mixture. Place the planks on the griddle and cover. Grill for about 15-20 minutes, until the salmon is cooked through. Garnish with fresh dill and serve.

Grilled Vegetable Platter

Servings: 4
Prep Time: 15 minutes
Cooking Time: 15 minutes
Description: A colorful and healthy assortment of grilled vegetables, perfect as a side dish or main course.
Ingredients:

- 2 zucchinis, sliced
- 2 bell peppers, sliced
- 1 red onion, sliced
- 1 eggplant, sliced
- 1/4 cup olive oil
- 2 tablespoons balsamic vinegar
- 3 cloves garlic, minced
- Salt and freshly ground black pepper
- Fresh basil, chopped for garnish

Preparation Steps:

In a bowl, combine olive oil, balsamic vinegar, garlic, salt, and pepper. Toss the vegetables in the marinade. Preheat your Blackstone griddle to medium-high heat. Grill the vegetables for about 5-7 minutes on each side until tender and slightly charred. Arrange the grilled vegetables on a platter and garnish with chopped fresh basil. Serve hot or at room temperature.

Beef Tenderloin with Red Wine Reduction

Servings: 4
Prep Time: 15 minutes
Cooking Time: 20 minutes
Description: Elegant beef tenderloin steaks cooked to perfection and served with a rich red wine reduction sauce.
Ingredients:

- 4 beef tenderloin steaks
- 2 tablespoons olive oil
- Salt and freshly ground black pepper

- 1 cup red wine
- 1/2 cup beef broth
- 2 shallots, minced
- 2 cloves garlic, minced
- 2 tablespoons butter
- Fresh thyme for garnish

Preparation Steps:

Preheat your Blackstone griddle to high heat. Season the beef tenderloin steaks with salt and pepper. Add olive oil to the griddle and sear the steaks for about 4-5 minutes on each side for medium-rare, adjusting the time for your preferred doneness. Remove the steaks from the griddle and let them rest. In a small saucepan, melt the butter over medium heat. Add the minced shallots and garlic, sautéing until soft. Pour in the red wine and beef broth, bringing the mixture to a simmer. Cook until the sauce reduces by half and thickens. Serve the beef tenderloin steaks with the red wine reduction sauce, garnished with fresh thyme.

Seafood Paella

Servings: 4
Prep Time: 20 minutes
Cooking Time: 30 minutes
Description: A vibrant and flavorful Spanish rice dish loaded with fresh seafood, vegetables, and aromatic spices.
Ingredients:

- 1 cup Arborio rice or paella rice
- 2 tablespoons olive oil
- 1 onion, finely chopped
- 1 red bell pepper, diced
- 3 cloves garlic, minced
- 1 teaspoon smoked paprika
- 1/2 teaspoon saffron threads (optional)
- 4 cups seafood or chicken broth
- 1/2 pound shrimp, peeled and deveined
- 1/2 pound mussels, scrubbed and debearded
- 1/2 pound squid rings
- 1 cup frozen peas
- Salt and freshly ground black pepper
- Lemon wedges for serving
- Fresh parsley, chopped for garnish

Preparation Steps:

Preheat your Blackstone griddle to medium-high heat. In a large paella pan or a wide skillet, heat the olive oil on the griddle. Add the chopped onion and red bell pepper, sautéing until soft. Stir in the minced garlic, smoked paprika, and saffron threads, cooking for another minute until fragrant. Add the rice and stir to coat it in the oil and spices. Pour in the broth, bring it to a simmer, and reduce the heat to medium. Cook the rice for about 15 minutes, stirring occasionally. Add the shrimp, mussels, squid, and peas, nestling them into the rice. Continue cooking for another 10-15 minutes, until the seafood is cooked through and the rice is tender. Season with salt and pepper to taste. Garnish with fresh parsley and serve with lemon wedges.

Pork Tenderloin with Apple Chutney

Servings: 4
Prep Time: 15 minutes
Cooking Time: 30 minutes
Description: Juicy pork tenderloin paired with a sweet and tangy apple chutney, creating a perfect harmony of flavors for a special dinner.
Ingredients:

- 2 pork tenderloins
- 2 tablespoons olive oil
- Salt and freshly ground black pepper
- 2 tablespoons Dijon mustard
- 1/4 cup brown sugar
- 1 teaspoon dried thyme

For the Apple Chutney:

- 2 apples, peeled, cored, and diced
- 1/2 cup onion, finely chopped
- 1/4 cup apple cider vinegar
- 1/4 cup brown sugar
- 1 teaspoon grated fresh ginger
- 1/4 teaspoon cinnamon
- 1/4 teaspoon ground cloves
- Salt and freshly ground black pepper

Preparation Steps:
Preheat your Blackstone griddle to medium-high heat. In a bowl, mix the olive oil, salt, pepper, Dijon mustard, brown sugar, and dried thyme. Rub the mixture over the pork tenderloins. Place the pork on the griddle and sear on all sides until browned, about 10 minutes. Reduce the heat to medium, cover the pork with foil, and continue to cook for another 15-20 minutes until the internal temperature reaches 145°F (63°C). Remove the pork from the griddle and let it rest for a few minutes before slicing.

While the pork is cooking, prepare the apple chutney. In a saucepan on the griddle, combine the diced apples, chopped onion, apple cider vinegar, brown sugar, grated ginger, cinnamon, cloves, salt, and pepper. Bring to a simmer and cook for about 10-15 minutes until the apples are soft and the mixture has thickened. Serve the sliced pork tenderloin with a generous spoonful of apple chutney on top. Garnish with fresh herbs if desired.

Chapter 9: Vegetarian and Special Diet Recipes

This chapter offers a variety of 12 dishes catering to vegetarian, vegan, gluten-free, and low-carb diets, ensuring everyone can enjoy delicious meals on the griddle.

Quinoa and Black Bean Stuffed Peppers

Servings: 4
Prep Time: 20 minutes
Cooking Time: 30 minutes
Description: Colorful bell peppers stuffed with a flavorful mixture of quinoa, black beans, and vegetables, making for a nutritious and satisfying vegetarian meal.
Ingredients:

- 4 large bell peppers
- 1 cup cooked quinoa
- 1 can (15 oz) black beans, rinsed and drained
- 1 cup corn kernels (fresh or frozen)
- 1 small onion, diced
- 1 cup diced tomatoes
- 1 teaspoon cumin
- 1 teaspoon chili powder
- Salt and freshly ground black pepper
- 1 cup shredded cheese (optional, for a non-vegan version)
- Fresh cilantro, chopped for garnish

Preparation Steps:
Preheat your Blackstone griddle to medium heat. Cut the tops off the bell peppers and remove the seeds. In a bowl, mix the cooked quinoa, black beans, corn, diced onion, tomatoes, cumin, chili powder, salt, and pepper. Stuff the bell peppers with the quinoa mixture. Place the stuffed peppers on the griddle and cover with a metal bowl or foil. Cook for about 25-30 minutes until the peppers are tender. If using cheese, sprinkle it over the top of the peppers in the last 5 minutes of cooking. Garnish with chopped cilantro and serve hot.

Vegan Chickpea Burgers

Servings: 4
Prep Time: 15 minutes
Cooking Time: 10 minutes
Description: Tasty and satisfying vegan burgers made from chickpeas, vegetables, and spices, perfect for a healthy and delicious lunch or dinner.
Ingredients:

- 1 can (15 oz) chickpeas, rinsed and drained
- 1/2 cup breadcrumbs (gluten-free if needed)
- 1 small carrot, grated
- 1 small zucchini, grated
- 2 cloves garlic, minced
- 1 tablespoon tahini
- 1 tablespoon soy sauce (or tamari for gluten-free)
- 1 teaspoon cumin
- Salt and freshly ground black pepper
- 2 tablespoons olive oil
- 4 burger buns (gluten-free if needed)
- Lettuce, tomato, and other desired toppings

Preparation Steps:

In a large bowl, mash the chickpeas until mostly smooth. Add the breadcrumbs, grated carrot, grated zucchini, garlic, tahini, soy sauce, cumin, salt, and pepper. Mix well until the ingredients are combined. Form the mixture into four patties. Preheat your Blackstone griddle to medium-high heat and add the olive oil. Cook the patties for about 4-5 minutes on each side, until golden brown and heated through. Toast the burger buns on the griddle until lightly browned. Assemble the burgers with lettuce, tomato, and your favorite toppings. Serve immediately.

Gluten-Free Grilled Pizza

Servings: 4
Prep Time: 15 minutes
Cooking Time: 10 minutes
Description: A delicious gluten-free pizza with a crispy crust, topped with your favorite sauce, cheese, and fresh ingredients.
Ingredients:

- 1 gluten-free pizza crust
- 1/2 cup pizza sauce
- 1 cup shredded mozzarella cheese (or dairy-free cheese for vegan)
- 1/2 cup sliced bell peppers
- 1/2 cup sliced mushrooms
- 1/4 cup sliced red onion
- Fresh basil leaves for garnish
- Olive oil for brushing

Preparation Steps:

Preheat your Blackstone griddle to medium-high heat. Brush one side of the gluten-free pizza crust with olive oil and place it oil-side down on the griddle. Cook for about 2-3 minutes until the bottom is crispy. Brush the top side with olive oil, then flip the crust. Spread the pizza sauce evenly over the crust, then sprinkle with shredded cheese. Add the sliced bell peppers, mushrooms, and red onion. Close the griddle lid or cover the pizza with a large metal bowl to melt the cheese. Cook for another 5-7 minutes until the cheese is bubbly and the crust is golden brown. Remove from the griddle, garnish with fresh basil leaves, and serve hot.

Low-Carb Cauliflower Fried Rice

Servings: 4
Prep Time: 10 minutes
Cooking Time: 10 minutes
Description: A healthy, low-carb alternative to traditional fried rice, made with riced cauliflower and packed with vegetables and flavor.
Ingredients:

- 1 large head of cauliflower, riced
- 1 cup frozen peas and carrots
- 1 small onion, diced
- 2 cloves garlic, minced
- 2 tablespoons soy sauce (or tamari for gluten-free)
- 2 tablespoons sesame oil
- 2 eggs, lightly beaten (omit for vegan)
- 2 green onions, sliced
- Salt and freshly ground black pepper
- Optional: tofu or cooked chicken for added protein

Preparation Steps:
Preheat your Blackstone griddle to medium-high heat and add the sesame oil. Add the diced onion and garlic, sautéing until fragrant and the onion is translucent. Add the riced cauliflower, frozen peas, and carrots. Cook for about 5-7 minutes, stirring frequently, until the vegetables are tender. Push the vegetables to one side of the griddle and pour the beaten eggs onto the other side, scrambling them until fully cooked. Mix the scrambled eggs into the cauliflower mixture. Add the soy sauce, green onions, salt, and pepper, stirring well to combine. Cook for another 2-3 minutes until everything is heated through. Serve hot, with optional tofu or cooked chicken for added protein.

Grilled Vegetable Skewers with Tofu

Servings: 4
Prep Time: 20 minutes
Cooking Time: 10 minutes
Description: Colorful vegetable skewers paired with marinated tofu, perfect for a light and nutritious meal.
Ingredients:

- 1 block firm tofu, drained and cubed
- 2 bell peppers, cut into chunks
- 1 zucchini, sliced
- 1 red onion, cut into chunks

- 8 cherry tomatoes
- 2 tablespoons olive oil
- 1 tablespoon soy sauce (or tamari for gluten-free)
- 1 teaspoon garlic powder
- 1 teaspoon onion powder
- Salt and freshly ground black pepper
- Wooden or metal skewers

Preparation Steps:

In a bowl, mix olive oil, soy sauce, garlic powder, onion powder, salt, and pepper. Add the tofu cubes and marinate for at least 15 minutes. Thread the tofu, bell peppers, zucchini, red onion, and cherry tomatoes onto skewers, alternating the ingredients. Preheat your Blackstone griddle to medium-high heat. Place the skewers on the griddle and cook for about 8-10 minutes, turning occasionally, until the vegetables are tender and slightly charred. Serve hot.

Spaghetti Squash with Pesto

Servings: 4
Prep Time: 10 minutes
Cooking Time: 40 minutes
Description: A delicious low-carb dish featuring roasted spaghetti squash tossed with fresh basil pesto.
Ingredients:

- 1 large spaghetti squash
- 2 tablespoons olive oil
- Salt and freshly ground black pepper
- 1 cup fresh basil pesto (store-bought or homemade)
- Cherry tomatoes, halved (optional)
- Grated Parmesan cheese (optional, for a non-vegan version)

Preparation Steps:

Preheat your oven to 400°F (200°C). Cut the spaghetti squash in half lengthwise and scoop out the seeds. Brush the inside of the squash with olive oil and season with salt and pepper. Place the squash halves cut side down on a baking sheet and roast for about 40 minutes, or until the flesh is tender and easily shredded with a fork. Let the squash cool slightly, then use a fork to scrape the flesh into spaghetti-like strands. In a large bowl, toss the spaghetti squash with the basil pesto. Add cherry tomatoes and grated Parmesan cheese if desired. Serve hot or at room temperature.

Zucchini Noodles with Avocado Sauce

Servings: 4
Prep Time: 15 minutes
Cooking Time: 5 minutes

Description: Fresh zucchini noodles tossed in a creamy avocado sauce, making for a healthy and satisfying meal.

Ingredients:

- 4 large zucchinis, spiralized into noodles
- 2 ripe avocados
- 1/4 cup fresh basil leaves
- 2 cloves garlic
- Juice of 1 lemon
- 2 tablespoons olive oil
- Salt and freshly ground black pepper
- Cherry tomatoes, halved (optional)

Preparation Steps:

In a food processor, combine the avocados, basil leaves, garlic, lemon juice, olive oil, salt, and pepper. Blend until smooth and creamy. Preheat your Blackstone griddle to medium heat. Add the zucchini noodles and cook for about 2-3 minutes, just until slightly tender. Remove from heat and toss with the avocado sauce. Add cherry tomatoes if desired. Serve immediately.

Grilled Eggplant Steaks

Servings: 4
Prep Time: 10 minutes
Cooking Time: 10 minutes
Description: Thick slices of eggplant marinated and grilled to perfection, served as a hearty vegetarian main dish.

Ingredients:

- 2 large eggplants, sliced into 1-inch thick steaks
- 1/4 cup olive oil
- 2 tablespoons balsamic vinegar
- 2 cloves garlic, minced
- 1 teaspoon dried oregano
- Salt and freshly ground black pepper
- Fresh parsley, chopped for garnish (optional)

Preparation Steps:

In a bowl, mix olive oil, balsamic vinegar, garlic, oregano, salt, and pepper. Brush the eggplant slices with the marinade and let them sit for at least 10 minutes. Preheat your Blackstone griddle to medium-high heat. Place the eggplant steaks on the griddle and cook for about 4-5 minutes on each side, until tender and slightly charred. Garnish with chopped fresh parsley if desired. Serve hot.

Vegan Grilled Cheese with Tomato Soup

Servings: 4
Prep Time: 15 minutes
Cooking Time: 20 minutes
Description: A comforting and classic combination of vegan grilled cheese sandwiches served with creamy tomato soup.
Ingredients:

- 8 slices of your favorite vegan bread
- 4 tablespoons vegan butter
- 8 slices vegan cheese
- 1 tablespoon olive oil
- 1 onion, diced
- 2 cloves garlic, minced
- 1 can (28 oz) crushed tomatoes
- 2 cups vegetable broth
- 1 teaspoon dried basil
- Salt and freshly ground black pepper
- Fresh basil leaves for garnish (optional)

Preparation Steps:
Preheat your Blackstone griddle to medium heat. Spread vegan butter on one side of each slice of bread. Place four slices of bread, buttered side down, on the griddle. Top each with two slices of vegan cheese and another slice of bread, buttered side up. Cook the sandwiches for about 3-4 minutes on each side, until golden brown and the cheese is melted. In a saucepan on the griddle, heat the olive oil and sauté the diced onion and garlic until soft. Add the crushed tomatoes, vegetable broth, dried basil, salt, and pepper. Bring to a simmer and cook for about 10-15 minutes, stirring occasionally. Use an immersion blender to blend the soup until smooth and creamy. Serve the grilled cheese sandwiches hot with a bowl of tomato soup, garnished with fresh basil leaves if desired.

Stuffed Portobello Mushrooms with Spinach and Artichoke

Servings: 4
Prep Time: 15 minutes
Cooking Time: 20 minutes
Description: Large portobello mushrooms stuffed with a creamy spinach and artichoke filling, then grilled to perfection.
Ingredients:

- 4 large portobello mushrooms
- 2 tablespoons olive oil
- 2 cloves garlic, minced

- 4 cups fresh spinach, chopped
- 1 cup canned artichoke hearts, drained and chopped
- 1/2 cup vegan cream cheese (or regular cream cheese for non-vegan)
- 1/4 cup nutritional yeast (or Parmesan cheese for non-vegan)
- Salt and freshly ground black pepper
- Fresh parsley, chopped for garnish

Preparation Steps:
Start by cleaning the portobello mushrooms with a damp cloth and removing the stems. In a pan, heat 1 tablespoon of olive oil over medium heat. Add the minced garlic and sauté until fragrant. Add the chopped spinach and artichoke hearts, cooking until the spinach is wilted. Stir in the vegan cream cheese and nutritional yeast, mixing until smooth and creamy. Season with salt and pepper to taste. Preheat your Blackstone griddle to medium-high heat. Brush the mushrooms with the remaining olive oil and place them on the griddle, gill side up. Cook for about 5 minutes, then flip and cook for another 5 minutes until tender. Fill each mushroom with the spinach and artichoke mixture, and cook for an additional 5 minutes until the filling is hot and slightly browned. Garnish with chopped fresh parsley and serve hot.

Grilled Sweet Potatoes with Black Bean Salsa

Servings: 4
Prep Time: 10 minutes
Cooking Time: 15 minutes
Description: Sweet potato slices grilled until tender and topped with a zesty black bean salsa, perfect for a healthy and flavorful meal.
Ingredients:

- 2 large sweet potatoes, sliced into 1/2-inch rounds
- 2 tablespoons olive oil
- Salt and freshly ground black pepper
- 1 can (15 oz) black beans, rinsed and drained
- 1 cup corn kernels (fresh or frozen)
- 1/2 cup red bell pepper, diced
- 1/4 cup red onion, finely chopped
- 1/4 cup fresh cilantro, chopped
- Juice of 1 lime
- 1 teaspoon ground cumin

Preparation Steps:
Preheat your Blackstone griddle to medium-high heat. Brush the sweet potato slices with olive oil and season with salt and pepper. Place the sweet potato slices on the griddle and cook for about 5-7 minutes on each side, until tender and grill marks appear. While the sweet potatoes are cooking, prepare the black bean salsa. In a bowl, combine the black beans, corn, red bell pepper, red onion, cilantro, lime juice, cumin, salt, and pepper. Mix

well. Once the sweet potatoes are cooked, transfer them to a serving platter and top with the black bean salsa. Serve immediately.

Keto-Friendly Grilled Cauliflower Steaks

Servings: 4
Prep Time: 10 minutes
Cooking Time: 15 minutes
Description: Thick slices of cauliflower grilled to perfection and served with a flavorful herb sauce, making for a satisfying low-carb and vegetarian meal.
Ingredients:

- 1 large cauliflower, cut into 1-inch thick steaks
- 3 tablespoons olive oil
- 2 cloves garlic, minced
- 1 teaspoon paprika
- 1 teaspoon dried thyme
- Salt and freshly ground black pepper
- 1/4 cup fresh parsley, chopped
- 2 tablespoons lemon juice

Preparation Steps:
Preheat your Blackstone griddle to medium-high heat. In a small bowl, mix the olive oil, minced garlic, paprika, dried thyme, salt, and pepper. Brush both sides of the cauliflower steaks with the seasoned olive oil. Place the cauliflower steaks on the griddle and cook for about 5-7 minutes on each side, until tender and charred. In a separate bowl, mix the chopped parsley and lemon juice. Once the cauliflower steaks are cooked, transfer them to a serving platter and drizzle with the parsley and lemon juice mixture. Serve hot and enjoy this healthy, keto-friendly vegetarian dish.

Chapter 10: Desserts and Breads

This chapter features 12 sweet treats and baked goods that can be made on a griddle, including cookies, fruit griddles, and flatbreads.

Griddle Chocolate Chip Cookies

Servings: 12 cookies
Prep Time: 15 minutes
Cooking Time: 10 minutes
Description: Soft and chewy chocolate chip cookies baked directly on your griddle, perfect for a quick and easy dessert.
Ingredients:

- 1/2 cup unsalted butter, softened
- 1/2 cup brown sugar
- 1/4 cup granulated sugar
- 1 egg
- 1 teaspoon vanilla extract
- 1 1/4 cups all-purpose flour
- 1/2 teaspoon baking soda
- 1/4 teaspoon salt
- 1 cup chocolate chips

Preparation Steps:
Preheat your Blackstone griddle to medium-low heat. In a bowl, cream together the butter, brown sugar, and granulated sugar until light and fluffy. Beat in the egg and vanilla extract. In another bowl, whisk together the flour, baking soda, and salt. Gradually add the dry ingredients to the wet mixture, stirring until just combined. Fold in the chocolate chips. Drop spoonfuls of dough onto the griddle, spacing them apart. Cook for about 5 minutes on each side, or until the cookies are golden brown and set. Let them cool slightly before serving.

Banana Pancakes

Servings: 4
Prep Time: 10 minutes
Cooking Time: 10 minutes
Description: Fluffy and sweet banana pancakes that are perfect for breakfast or a delightful treat any time of the day.
Ingredients:

- 1 cup all-purpose flour
- 2 tablespoons sugar
- 1 teaspoon baking powder

- 1/2 teaspoon baking soda
- 1/4 teaspoon salt
- 1 cup buttermilk
- 1 large egg
- 2 tablespoons melted butter
- 2 ripe bananas, mashed
- Butter for griddling

Preparation Steps:

In a large bowl, whisk together the flour, sugar, baking powder, baking soda, and salt. In another bowl, mix the buttermilk, egg, melted butter, and mashed bananas. Pour the wet ingredients into the dry ingredients and stir until just combined. Preheat your Blackstone griddle to medium heat and lightly butter it. Pour 1/4 cup of batter for each pancake onto the griddle. Cook until bubbles form on the surface, then flip and cook until golden brown. Serve hot with syrup and additional banana slices if desired.

Cinnamon Sugar Griddled Apples

Servings: 4
Prep Time: 10 minutes
Cooking Time: 10 minutes
Description: Sweet and tender apple slices coated in cinnamon sugar and cooked on the griddle, perfect as a dessert or topping for pancakes.
Ingredients:

- 4 apples, cored and sliced
- 2 tablespoons butter
- 1/4 cup granulated sugar
- 1 teaspoon ground cinnamon

Preparation Steps:

In a small bowl, mix the sugar and cinnamon together. Preheat your Blackstone griddle to medium heat and melt the butter on it. Add the apple slices and cook for about 5 minutes, turning occasionally, until they start to soften. Sprinkle the cinnamon sugar mixture over the apples and continue to cook for another 5 minutes, until the apples are tender and caramelized. Serve warm, either on their own or as a topping for pancakes or ice cream.

Blueberry Griddle Cakes

Servings: 4
Prep Time: 10 minutes
Cooking Time: 10 minutes
Description: Light and fluffy griddle cakes studded with juicy blueberries, perfect for a sweet breakfast or brunch.
Ingredients:

- 1 cup all-purpose flour
- 1 tablespoon sugar
- 1 teaspoon baking powder
- 1/2 teaspoon baking soda
- 1/4 teaspoon salt
- 1 cup buttermilk
- 1 large egg
- 2 tablespoons melted butter
- 1 cup fresh or frozen blueberries
- Butter for griddling

Preparation Steps:
In a large bowl, whisk together the flour, sugar, baking powder, baking soda, and salt. In another bowl, mix the buttermilk, egg, and melted butter. Pour the wet ingredients into the dry ingredients and stir until just combined. Gently fold in the blueberries. Preheat your Blackstone griddle to medium heat and lightly butter it. Pour 1/4 cup of batter for each griddle cake onto the griddle. Cook until bubbles form on the surface, then flip and cook until golden brown. Serve hot with syrup and extra blueberries if desired.

Griddled Peaches with Honey

Servings: 4
Prep Time: 5 minutes
Cooking Time: 5 minutes
Description: Juicy peaches caramelized on the griddle and drizzled with honey, perfect as a dessert or a sweet side dish.
Ingredients:

- 4 ripe peaches, halved and pitted
- 2 tablespoons butter
- 2 tablespoons honey
- Optional: vanilla ice cream for serving

Preparation Steps:
Preheat your Blackstone griddle to medium-high heat and melt the butter on it. Place the peach halves cut side down on the griddle and cook for about 2-3 minutes, until they are caramelized and softened. Flip the peaches and cook for another 2 minutes. Remove from the griddle and drizzle with honey. Serve warm, optionally with a scoop of vanilla ice cream.

Nutella-Stuffed Pancakes

Servings: 4
Prep Time: 15 minutes
Cooking Time: 10 minutes
Description: Fluffy pancakes with a delicious Nutella center, perfect for a decadent

breakfast or dessert.

Ingredients:

- 1 cup all-purpose flour
- 2 tablespoons sugar
- 1 teaspoon baking powder
- 1/2 teaspoon baking soda
- 1/4 teaspoon salt
- 1 cup buttermilk
- 1 large egg
- 2 tablespoons melted butter
- 1/2 cup Nutella
- Butter for griddling

Preparation Steps:

In a large bowl, whisk together the flour, sugar, baking powder, baking soda, and salt. In another bowl, mix the buttermilk, egg, and melted butter. Pour the wet ingredients into the dry ingredients and stir until just combined. Preheat your Blackstone griddle to medium heat and lightly butter it. Drop 1/4 cup of batter onto the griddle for each pancake. Quickly add a spoonful of Nutella in the center of each pancake, then cover with a little more batter. Cook until bubbles form on the surface, then flip and cook until golden brown. Serve hot with additional Nutella if desired.

Griddle Scones

Servings: 8
Prep Time: 15 minutes
Cooking Time: 10 minutes
Description: Soft and fluffy scones cooked on the griddle, perfect for breakfast or an afternoon tea.

Ingredients:

- 2 cups all-purpose flour
- 1/4 cup sugar
- 1 tablespoon baking powder
- 1/2 teaspoon salt
- 1/2 cup cold unsalted butter, cubed
- 2/3 cup buttermilk
- 1 teaspoon vanilla extract
- Optional: dried fruits, chocolate chips, or nuts

Preparation Steps:

In a large bowl, whisk together the flour, sugar, baking powder, and salt. Cut in the cold butter until the mixture resembles coarse crumbs. Stir in the buttermilk and vanilla extract until just combined. If using, fold in dried fruits, chocolate chips, or nuts. Preheat your Blackstone griddle to medium heat. Divide the dough into 8 equal portions and shape each into a round. Place the scones on the griddle and cook for about 5 minutes on each side, until golden brown and cooked through. Serve warm with butter and jam.

Lemon Poppy Seed Flatbread

Servings: 4
Prep Time: 10 minutes
Cooking Time: 10 minutes
Description: A delightful flatbread flavored with lemon and poppy seeds, perfect as a snack or side dish.
Ingredients:

- 2 cups all-purpose flour
- 1 teaspoon baking powder
- 1/2 teaspoon salt
- 1/2 cup water
- 1/4 cup olive oil
- Zest of 1 lemon
- 1 tablespoon poppy seeds
- Additional olive oil for brushing

Preparation Steps:

In a large bowl, combine the flour, baking powder, and salt. Stir in the water, olive oil, lemon zest, and poppy seeds until a dough forms. Divide the dough into 4 equal portions and roll each into a thin flatbread. Preheat your Blackstone griddle to medium-high heat. Brush each flatbread with olive oil and place on the griddle. Cook for about 2-3 minutes on each side until golden brown and slightly crispy. Serve warm.

Pumpkin Spice Griddle Cakes

Servings: 4
Prep Time: 10 minutes
Cooking Time: 10 minutes
Description: Fluffy griddle cakes infused with pumpkin spice, perfect for a cozy autumn breakfast.
Ingredients:

- 1 cup all-purpose flour
- 2 tablespoons sugar
- 1 teaspoon baking powder
- 1/2 teaspoon baking soda
- 1/4 teaspoon salt
- 1 teaspoon pumpkin pie spice
- 1 cup buttermilk
- 1/2 cup pumpkin puree
- 1 large egg
- 2 tablespoons melted butter
- Butter for griddling

Preparation Steps:

In a large bowl, whisk together the flour, sugar, baking powder, baking soda, salt, and pumpkin pie spice. In another bowl, mix the buttermilk, pumpkin puree, egg, and melted butter. Pour the wet ingredients into the dry ingredients and stir until just combined. Preheat your Blackstone griddle to medium heat and lightly butter it. Pour 1/4 cup of batter for each griddle cake onto the griddle. Cook until bubbles form on the surface, then flip and cook until golden brown. Serve hot with syrup and a sprinkle of cinnamon if desired.

Griddled Pineapple with Caramel Sauce

Servings: 4
Prep Time: 10 minutes
Cooking Time: 10 minutes
Description: Juicy pineapple slices caramelized on the griddle and drizzled with a rich caramel sauce, perfect for a delightful dessert.
Ingredients:

- 1 fresh pineapple, peeled, cored, and sliced
- 2 tablespoons butter
- 1/2 cup sugar
- 1/4 cup heavy cream
- 1 teaspoon vanilla extract
- Pinch of salt

Preparation Steps:

Preheat your Blackstone griddle to medium-high heat. In a saucepan on the griddle, melt the butter and sugar together, stirring until the sugar dissolves and begins to caramelize. Slowly add the heavy cream, vanilla extract, and salt, stirring continuously until smooth and well combined. Set the caramel sauce aside. Place the pineapple slices on the griddle and cook for about 2-3 minutes on each side, until they are golden brown and caramelized. Remove the pineapple from the griddle and drizzle with the warm caramel sauce. Serve immediately.

Chocolate Banana Flatbread

Servings: 4
Prep Time: 10 minutes
Cooking Time: 5 minutes
Description: Sweet flatbread topped with sliced bananas and melted chocolate, perfect for a quick and indulgent treat.
Ingredients:

- 4 flatbreads
- 1/2 cup chocolate chips or chopped chocolate
- 2 bananas, sliced

- 2 tablespoons butter
- 1 tablespoon powdered sugar (optional)

Preparation Steps:

Preheat your Blackstone griddle to medium heat and lightly butter it. Place the flatbreads on the griddle and cook for about 1-2 minutes on each side until warmed and slightly crispy. Remove from heat and immediately sprinkle with chocolate chips. Let the chocolate melt slightly, then spread it evenly over the flatbreads. Top with sliced bananas. If desired, sprinkle with powdered sugar before serving. Serve warm.

Griddled Berry Compote

Servings: 4
Prep Time: 5 minutes
Cooking Time: 10 minutes
Description: A delicious and versatile berry compote that can be served over pancakes, waffles, or ice cream.
Ingredients:

- 2 cups mixed berries (such as strawberries, blueberries, raspberries, and blackberries)
- 1/4 cup sugar
- 1 tablespoon lemon juice
- 1 teaspoon vanilla extract

Preparation Steps:

Preheat your Blackstone griddle to medium heat. In a saucepan on the griddle, combine the mixed berries, sugar, and lemon juice. Cook, stirring occasionally, until the berries release their juices and the mixture thickens, about 10 minutes. Stir in the vanilla extract and cook for an additional minute. Remove from heat and let cool slightly. Serve the berry compote warm over pancakes, waffles, or ice cream, or store in an airtight container in the refrigerator for up to a week.

Chapter 11: World Cuisine on Your Griddle

This chapter explores 12 international recipes that adapt well to griddle cooking, including dishes like fajitas, stir-fries, and crepes.

Mexican Fajitas

Servings: 4
Prep Time: 15 minutes
Cooking Time: 10 minutes
Description: Sizzling strips of marinated steak or chicken cooked with bell peppers and onions, served with warm tortillas and toppings.
Ingredients:

- 1 pound flank steak or chicken breast, sliced into strips
- 2 bell peppers, sliced
- 1 large onion, sliced
- 2 tablespoons olive oil
- 1 tablespoon lime juice
- 2 teaspoons chili powder
- 1 teaspoon cumin
- Salt and freshly ground black pepper
- Warm tortillas for serving
- Optional toppings: salsa, guacamole, sour cream, shredded cheese, chopped cilantro

Preparation Steps:
In a bowl, combine olive oil, lime juice, chili powder, cumin, salt, and pepper. Add the steak or chicken strips, bell peppers, and onions, tossing to coat evenly. Preheat your Blackstone griddle to medium-high heat. Add the mixture to the griddle and cook for about 8-10 minutes, stirring occasionally, until the meat is cooked through and the vegetables are tender. Serve the fajitas hot with warm tortillas and your favorite toppings.

Japanese Yakisoba

Servings: 4
Prep Time: 15 minutes
Cooking Time: 10 minutes
Description: A popular Japanese stir-fried noodle dish with pork, vegetables, and a savory sauce.
Ingredients:

- 1 pound pork belly or pork loin, thinly sliced

- 4 cups cabbage, chopped
- 1 large carrot, julienned
- 1 onion, sliced
- 3 packages yakisoba noodles, pre-cooked
- 1/4 cup soy sauce
- 2 tablespoons Worcestershire sauce
- 1 tablespoon oyster sauce
- 2 tablespoons vegetable oil
- Salt and freshly ground black pepper
- Optional: pickled ginger for garnish

Preparation Steps:

Preheat your Blackstone griddle to medium-high heat and add vegetable oil. Cook the pork slices until browned and cooked through, about 5 minutes. Add the cabbage, carrot, and onion, stirring frequently, and cook for another 5 minutes until the vegetables are tender. Add the yakisoba noodles and toss to combine. Stir in the soy sauce, Worcestershire sauce, and oyster sauce, mixing well. Cook for another 2-3 minutes until everything is heated through. Serve hot, garnished with pickled ginger if desired.

Italian Panini

Servings: 4
Prep Time: 10 minutes
Cooking Time: 10 minutes
Description: Crispy grilled sandwiches filled with your choice of Italian meats, cheeses, and vegetables.
Ingredients:

- 8 slices ciabatta or sourdough bread
- 8 slices provolone or mozzarella cheese
- 4 ounces sliced prosciutto or salami
- 1 large tomato, sliced
- Fresh basil leaves
- 2 tablespoons olive oil
- Optional: balsamic glaze for drizzling

Preparation Steps:

Preheat your Blackstone griddle to medium heat. Assemble the panini by layering cheese, prosciutto or salami, tomato slices, and basil leaves between two slices of bread. Brush the outside of each sandwich with olive oil. Place the sandwiches on the griddle and press down with a heavy spatula or grill press. Cook for about 4-5 minutes on each side until the bread is golden brown and the cheese is melted. Serve hot, drizzled with balsamic glaze if desired.

Korean Bulgogi

Servings: 4
Prep Time: 20 minutes
Cooking Time: 10 minutes
Description: Tender slices of beef marinated in a sweet and savory sauce, then grilled to perfection, served with rice and kimchi.
Ingredients:

- 1 pound beef sirloin, thinly sliced
- 1/4 cup soy sauce
- 2 tablespoons sugar
- 2 tablespoons sesame oil
- 2 cloves garlic, minced
- 1 tablespoon grated ginger
- 1/2 pear, grated
- 1 onion, thinly sliced
- 1 tablespoon sesame seeds
- 2 green onions, chopped
- Cooked rice for serving
- Kimchi for serving

Preparation Steps:
In a bowl, mix soy sauce, sugar, sesame oil, garlic, ginger, grated pear, and onion. Add the beef slices and marinate for at least 30 minutes. Preheat your Blackstone griddle to medium-high heat. Add the marinated beef and onions to the griddle and cook for about 5-7 minutes, stirring frequently, until the beef is cooked through and slightly caramelized. Sprinkle with sesame seeds and chopped green onions. Serve hot with cooked rice and kimchi.

French Crepes

Servings: 4
Prep Time: 15 minutes
Cooking Time: 15 minutes
Description: Delicate and thin French pancakes that can be filled with sweet or savory fillings.
Ingredients:

- 1 cup all-purpose flour
- 2 eggs
- 1/2 cup milk
- 1/2 cup water
- 1/4 teaspoon salt
- 2 tablespoons butter, melted
- Sweet or savory fillings (e.g., Nutella, strawberries, ham, cheese)

Preparation Steps:

In a large bowl, whisk together the flour and eggs. Gradually add the milk and water, stirring to combine. Add the salt and melted butter, whisking until smooth. Preheat your Blackstone griddle to medium heat and lightly grease it with butter. Pour 1/4 cup of batter onto the griddle and spread it out thinly using a spatula. Cook for about 2 minutes, until the edges start to lift and the crepe is lightly browned. Flip and cook for another 1-2 minutes. Remove the crepe from the griddle and fill with your desired fillings. Fold or roll the crepe and serve immediately. Repeat with the remaining batter.

Thai Pad Thai

Servings: 4
Prep Time: 15 minutes
Cooking Time: 10 minutes
Description: A classic Thai stir-fried noodle dish with shrimp, tofu, eggs, and a tangy tamarind sauce, topped with peanuts and lime.
Ingredients:

- 8 ounces rice noodles
- 1/2 pound shrimp, peeled and deveined
- 1/2 cup firm tofu, cubed
- 2 eggs, lightly beaten
- 1 cup bean sprouts
- 2 green onions, chopped
- 2 tablespoons vegetable oil
- 3 tablespoons tamarind paste
- 2 tablespoons fish sauce
- 1 tablespoon soy sauce
- 1 tablespoon brown sugar
- 1/4 cup roasted peanuts, chopped
- Lime wedges for serving
- Fresh cilantro for garnish

Preparation Steps:

Soak the rice noodles in hot water for 10 minutes, then drain and set aside. Preheat your Blackstone griddle to medium-high heat and add the vegetable oil. Cook the shrimp until pink and cooked through, about 3 minutes. Add the tofu and cook until golden brown. Push the shrimp and tofu to one side of the griddle and add the beaten eggs, scrambling until cooked through. Add the noodles to the griddle along with the tamarind paste, fish sauce, soy sauce, and brown sugar. Toss everything together until well combined. Stir in the bean sprouts and green onions, cooking for another 2-3 minutes. Serve hot, garnished with chopped peanuts, lime wedges, and fresh cilantro.

Indian Tandoori Chicken

Servings: 4
Prep Time: 20 minutes
Cooking Time: 20 minutes
Description: Spiced and marinated chicken grilled to perfection, served with naan or rice and a cooling yogurt sauce.
Ingredients:

- 4 boneless, skinless chicken breasts
- 1 cup plain yogurt
- 2 tablespoons lemon juice
- 2 tablespoons tandoori masala
- 1 tablespoon grated ginger
- 2 cloves garlic, minced
- 1 teaspoon ground cumin
- 1 teaspoon ground coriander
- 1/2 teaspoon turmeric
- 1/2 teaspoon cayenne pepper
- Salt and freshly ground black pepper
- Fresh cilantro for garnish
- Naan or rice for serving
- Yogurt sauce for serving

Preparation Steps:
In a bowl, mix the yogurt, lemon juice, tandoori masala, ginger, garlic, cumin, coriander, turmeric, cayenne pepper, salt, and pepper. Add the chicken breasts and coat them well in the marinade. Let marinate for at least 30 minutes. Preheat your Blackstone griddle to medium-high heat. Place the marinated chicken on the griddle and cook for about 6-8 minutes on each side, until the chicken is cooked through and has a nice char. Serve hot, garnished with fresh cilantro, alongside naan or rice and a yogurt sauce.

Greek Gyros

Servings: 4
Prep Time: 15 minutes
Cooking Time: 10 minutes
Description: Savory grilled meat wrapped in warm pita bread, topped with tzatziki sauce, tomatoes, onions, and lettuce.
Ingredients:

- 1 pound lamb or chicken, thinly sliced
- 2 tablespoons olive oil
- 2 cloves garlic, minced
- 1 teaspoon dried oregano
- 1 teaspoon ground cumin
- Salt and freshly ground black pepper

- 4 pita breads
- 1 cup tzatziki sauce
- 1 cup chopped tomatoes
- 1/2 cup sliced red onion
- 1 cup shredded lettuce

Preparation Steps:

In a bowl, combine the olive oil, garlic, oregano, cumin, salt, and pepper. Add the sliced lamb or chicken and mix well. Preheat your Blackstone griddle to medium-high heat. Cook the meat for about 5-7 minutes, stirring occasionally, until it is cooked through and slightly crispy. Warm the pita breads on the griddle for about 1 minute on each side. To assemble the gyros, spread tzatziki sauce on each pita, then top with the grilled meat, chopped tomatoes, sliced red onion, and shredded lettuce. Serve immediately.

Spanish Paella

Servings: 4
Prep Time: 20 minutes
Cooking Time: 30 minutes
Description: A flavorful Spanish rice dish loaded with seafood, chicken, and vegetables, cooked to perfection on the griddle.
Ingredients:

- 1 cup Arborio rice
- 1/2 pound shrimp, peeled and deveined
- 1/2 pound mussels, scrubbed and debearded
- 1/2 pound chicken thighs, cut into pieces
- 1 red bell pepper, diced
- 1 onion, diced
- 2 cloves garlic, minced
- 1 cup diced tomatoes
- 3 cups chicken broth
- 1/2 teaspoon saffron threads (optional)
- 1 teaspoon smoked paprika
- 2 tablespoons olive oil
- Salt and freshly ground black pepper
- Fresh parsley for garnish
- Lemon wedges for serving

Preparation Steps:

Preheat your Blackstone griddle to medium-high heat and add the olive oil. Cook the chicken pieces until browned and cooked through, then add the diced onion, red bell pepper, and garlic, sautéing until softened. Add the Arborio rice and cook for about 2 minutes, stirring to coat the rice with oil. Stir in the diced tomatoes, chicken broth, saffron threads (if using), smoked paprika, salt, and pepper. Reduce the heat to medium and let the mixture simmer for about 15 minutes, stirring occasionally. Add the shrimp and mussels, nestling them into the rice, and continue cooking until the seafood is cooked through and the rice is tender, about 10 more minutes. Garnish with fresh parsley and serve with lemon wedges.

Chinese Fried Rice

Servings: 4
Prep Time: 15 minutes
Cooking Time: 10 minutes
Description: A classic Chinese dish of stir-fried rice with vegetables, eggs, and optional protein, seasoned with soy sauce and sesame oil.
Ingredients:

- 4 cups cooked and cooled rice
- 2 tablespoons vegetable oil
- 2 cloves garlic, minced
- 1 small onion, diced
- 1 cup frozen peas and carrots, thawed
- 2 eggs, lightly beaten
- 3 tablespoons soy sauce
- 1 tablespoon sesame oil
- 1/4 cup chopped green onions
- Optional: diced chicken, shrimp, or tofu

Preparation Steps:
Preheat your Blackstone griddle to medium-high heat and add the vegetable oil. Sauté the garlic and onion until fragrant and translucent. Add the peas and carrots, and optional protein if using, and cook for about 3 minutes. Push the vegetables to the side and pour the beaten eggs onto the griddle, scrambling until fully cooked. Add the cooked rice and stir everything together, breaking up any clumps. Pour the soy sauce and sesame oil over the rice, stirring to combine and heat through. Garnish with chopped green onions and serve hot.

Argentinian Choripán

Servings: 4
Prep Time: 10 minutes
Cooking Time: 10 minutes
Description: A popular Argentinian sandwich made with grilled chorizo sausage, crusty bread, and chimichurri sauce.
Ingredients:

- 4 chorizo sausages
- 4 crusty rolls or baguettes
- 1 cup chimichurri sauce
- 1 red onion, thinly sliced
- Fresh cilantro for garnish

Preparation Steps:

Preheat your Blackstone griddle to medium-high heat. Grill the chorizo sausages for about 4-5 minutes on each side, until fully cooked and slightly charred. Cut the rolls or baguettes lengthwise and lightly toast them on the griddle. To assemble the sandwiches, place a grilled chorizo sausage in each roll, top with chimichurri sauce and sliced red onion. Garnish with fresh cilantro and serve immediately.

Vietnamese Banh Mi

Servings: 4
Prep Time: 15 minutes
Cooking Time: 10 minutes
Description: A Vietnamese sandwich with marinated pork, pickled vegetables, fresh herbs, and a spicy mayonnaise, served in a crispy baguette.
Ingredients:

- 1 pound pork tenderloin, thinly sliced
- 2 tablespoons soy sauce
- 2 tablespoons fish sauce
- 1 tablespoon sugar
- 2 cloves garlic, minced
- 1 teaspoon black pepper
- 4 baguettes
- 1 cup pickled carrots and daikon
- 1 cucumber, thinly sliced
- 1 jalapeño, thinly sliced
- Fresh cilantro
- 1/4 cup mayonnaise
- 1 tablespoon Sriracha sauce

Preparation Steps:

In a bowl, combine the soy sauce, fish sauce, sugar, garlic, and black pepper. Add the sliced pork and marinate for at least 15 minutes. Preheat your Blackstone griddle to medium-high heat and cook the marinated pork for about 5-7 minutes, until fully cooked and slightly caramelized. Cut the baguettes lengthwise and lightly toast them on the griddle. In a small bowl, mix the mayonnaise and Sriracha sauce. To assemble the sandwiches, spread the spicy mayonnaise on one side of each baguette, layer with cooked pork, pickled carrots and daikon, cucumber slices, jalapeño slices, and fresh cilantro. Serve immediately.

Part III: Mastering the Art of Griddle Cooking

Chapter 12: Troubleshooting Common Issues

This chapter provides solutions to common problems encountered during griddle cooking, such as uneven heating, sticking food, and flare-ups.

Uneven Heating
Solution: Ensure the griddle is preheated properly before cooking. Check for any blockages in the burners and clean them regularly. Use a griddle wind guard to prevent wind from affecting the heat distribution.

Sticking Food
Solution: Season your griddle well before first use and periodically thereafter. Use a generous amount of oil when cooking and ensure the griddle is adequately preheated. Clean the griddle surface after each use to maintain its non-stick properties.

Flare-Ups
Solution: Keep a spray bottle of water handy to quickly douse any flare-ups. Avoid cooking overly fatty foods directly on the griddle. Trim excess fat from meats and keep an eye on the temperature to prevent grease from igniting.

Food Burning
Solution: Control the griddle temperature by using a thermometer to ensure it stays within the optimal range for the food you're cooking. Use indirect heat for slower cooking and avoid overcrowding the griddle surface.

Rust Formation
Solution: After cooking, clean the griddle thoroughly and apply a thin layer of oil to the surface to protect it from moisture. Store the griddle in a dry place and use a cover to protect it from the elements.

Uneven Cooking
Solution: Rotate the food periodically to ensure even cooking. Use a griddle press for foods like burgers and sandwiches to ensure even contact with the griddle surface.

Maintaining Proper Temperature
Solution: Invest in an infrared thermometer to accurately measure the griddle surface temperature. Adjust the heat settings as needed and allow the griddle to come back to temperature between batches of food.

Cleaning Challenges

Solution: Use a griddle scraper to remove food residue after each cooking session. For tougher stains, use a mixture of water and vinegar or a specialized griddle cleaner. Regular maintenance will make cleaning easier over time.

Propane Issues

Solution: Ensure the propane tank is not empty and the connections are secure. Check for leaks using soapy water and replace any damaged hoses or fittings.

Wind and Weather Problems

Solution: Use a wind guard to protect the flame from being blown out. Cook in a sheltered area to minimize the effects of wind and weather on the griddle's performance.

Inconsistent Ignition

Solution: Regularly clean the igniter and burner area to ensure proper sparking. Replace the igniter battery if necessary and check the gas flow to ensure it is uninterrupted.

Warping Griddle Surface

Solution: Avoid sudden temperature changes, such as pouring cold water on a hot griddle. Allow the griddle to cool down gradually after use and ensure it is properly supported on a level surface.

BONUS CHAPTER: Pro Grilling and Cooking Tips

This bonus chapter is designed as a resource for enhancing your grilling skills and ensuring that every meal prepared on your Blackstone outdoor gas griddle is a culinary success. Here, you'll find expert advice, insider tricks, and seasoned techniques gathered from professional chefs and griddle enthusiasts alike.

Efficient Heat Management: Strategies for Mastering the Heat Zones on Your Griddle to Cook Multiple Dishes Simultaneously

One of the key skills in griddle cooking is efficient heat management. Mastering the heat zones on your griddle allows you to cook multiple dishes simultaneously, ensuring everything is cooked to perfection and ready to serve at the same time. Here are some strategies to help you achieve this:

Understanding Your Griddle's Heat Zones
Your Blackstone griddle likely has multiple burners, each capable of creating its own heat zone. Typically, the griddle will have a high heat zone near the center and lower heat zones towards the edges. Familiarize yourself with these zones by turning on the burners and using an infrared thermometer to measure the temperature in different areas. This will help you understand where the hottest and coolest spots are.

Preheating and Heat Adjustment
Always preheat your griddle before cooking. Turn on all burners to high and let the griddle heat up for 10-15 minutes. Once it's hot, adjust the burners to create different heat zones. For instance, you can set one side to high heat for searing meats, the middle to medium heat for cooking vegetables, and the other side to low heat for keeping food warm.

Utilizing the Heat Zones

- **High Heat Zone:** This area is perfect for searing steaks, burgers, and other meats that require a quick, high-temperature cook. Searing locks in the juices and creates a flavorful crust.
- **Medium Heat Zone:** Use this zone for cooking vegetables, eggs, and fish. The medium heat ensures that these foods cook evenly without burning.
- **Low Heat Zone:** This area is ideal for toasting buns, warming tortillas, or keeping cooked food warm while you finish other dishes.

Rotating and Moving Food
Don't be afraid to move food around the griddle as you cook. Start by searing meats on the high heat zone, then move them to medium or low heat to finish cooking. This method ensures that the exterior is nicely browned while the interior reaches the desired

doneness. Similarly, start vegetables on medium heat and move them to low heat once they are tender.

Zone Cooking for Multiple Dishes

When cooking a meal with multiple components, plan your cooking sequence to make the most of your griddle's heat zones. For example, sear your steaks on high heat first, then move them to low heat. Use the medium heat zone to cook vegetables while the steaks finish. This way, everything is ready at the same time without overcooking or burning.

Adjusting for Weather Conditions

Weather can affect your griddle's performance. On windy days, use wind guards to protect the flame and maintain consistent heat. In cold weather, preheat the griddle longer and use higher settings to compensate for heat loss.

Using Heat-Resistant Tools

Invest in heat-resistant tools like spatulas, tongs, and gloves. These tools allow you to manage food across different heat zones without the risk of burns or damage.

By understanding and managing the heat zones on your griddle, you can cook multiple dishes simultaneously, ensuring each one is perfectly prepared and ready to serve at the same time. This skill is essential for any griddle chef looking to elevate their cooking game.

Flavor Enhancements: Tips on How to Use Wood Chips for Smoking on the Griddle, Choosing the Best Oils for High-Heat Cooking, and Making Homemade Marinades That Enhance Flavor Without Burning

Enhancing the flavor of your dishes can take your griddle cooking to the next level. Here are some expert tips on how to use wood chips for smoking, choosing the best oils for high-heat cooking, and making homemade marinades that enhance flavor without burning.

Using Wood Chips for Smoking on the Griddle

Smoking adds a rich, complex flavor to meats and vegetables that can't be achieved with traditional grilling alone. To effectively use wood chips on your griddle, start by choosing the right wood chips. Different wood chips impart different flavors: apple and cherry wood provide a sweet, mild smoke, while hickory and mesquite offer stronger, more intense flavors. Select based on your preference and the type of food you're cooking. Soak the wood chips in water for at least 30 minutes before using them to help them smolder and produce smoke rather than burn quickly. Create a smoking pouch by placing the soaked wood chips in a small aluminum foil pouch and poke a few holes in the top to allow the smoke to escape. Position the foil pouch directly on one of the burners under the griddle, turning the burner to high until the chips start to smoke, then reducing the heat to maintain a steady smoke. Finally, place your food on the griddle, keeping the lid closed as much as possible to trap the smoke, and adjust the heat zones as needed to ensure even cooking and avoid burning.

Choosing the Best Oils for High-Heat Cooking

Not all oils are created equal, especially when it comes to high-heat cooking on a griddle. Some of the best oils to use include avocado oil, which has a high smoke point of around 520°F and a neutral flavor that won't overpower your food. Grapeseed oil is another great option with a high smoke point of around 420°F; it is light and versatile, making it perfect for searing and frying. Peanut oil is known for its high smoke point of about 450°F, ideal for grilling and frying, and adds a slight nutty flavor to your dishes. Refined coconut oil, with a smoke point of around 450°F, is also suitable for high-heat cooking and adds a subtle coconut flavor that pairs well with many dishes.

Making Homemade Marinades That Enhance Flavor Without Burning

Marinades can add incredible depth of flavor to your food. A good marinade typically includes an acidic component like lemon juice or vinegar and oil. The acid helps tenderize the meat, while the oil ensures even cooking and adds moisture. Avoid sugary marinades as sugar can burn quickly on high heat, leading to a charred exterior. If you want a sweet element, use honey or brown sugar sparingly and apply it towards the end of the cooking process. Fresh herbs and spices add vibrant flavors to your marinade; garlic, rosemary, thyme, and paprika are excellent choices. Marinate meats like chicken and beef for at least 30 minutes to a few hours, while fish and seafood require less time, usually around 15-30 minutes. Before cooking, remove excess marinade from the surface of your food to prevent burning and ensure a nice sear.

Example Marinade Recipe: Combine 1/4 cup olive oil, 2 tablespoons lemon juice, 3 cloves garlic (minced), 1 tablespoon fresh rosemary (chopped), 1 teaspoon smoked paprika, salt, and freshly ground black pepper in a bowl. Add your choice of meat, ensuring it's well coated. Marinate in the refrigerator for the appropriate amount of time, then pat dry and cook on the griddle.

By using these techniques, you can significantly enhance the flavor of your dishes, making every meal on your Blackstone griddle a memorable culinary experience.

Perfect Timing: Guidelines on the Optimal Cooking Times for a Variety of Foods, Ensuring Everything from Delicate Fish to Hearty Steaks is Cooked to Perfection

Achieving perfect timing on your griddle ensures that every dish, from delicate fish to hearty steaks, is cooked to perfection. Here are some guidelines to help you get it right every time.

Steaks and Burgers
For a medium-rare steak, cook a 1-inch thick steak for about 4-5 minutes per side on high heat. Adjust the time slightly for thicker or thinner cuts, and use an instant-read

thermometer to ensure an internal temperature of 130°F to 135°F. Burgers typically need about 4-5 minutes per side on medium-high heat, with an internal temperature of 160°F for ground beef.

Chicken

Boneless, skinless chicken breasts should be cooked on medium-high heat for 6-7 minutes per side. Check for an internal temperature of 165°F to ensure they are fully cooked. Bone-in chicken pieces take longer, around 10-12 minutes per side, and also need to reach 165°F internally.

Fish and Seafood

Delicate fish fillets like tilapia or sole should be cooked on medium heat for about 3-4 minutes per side. Thicker fillets like salmon or halibut need around 5-6 minutes per side. Shrimp cook very quickly, needing only 2-3 minutes per side on medium-high heat until they are pink and opaque. Scallops should be seared on high heat for about 2-3 minutes per side until they are golden brown.

Vegetables

Softer vegetables like bell peppers, zucchini, and mushrooms cook quickly, needing about 5-7 minutes on medium heat, turning occasionally. Harder vegetables like carrots or potatoes should be par-cooked or thinly sliced to ensure even cooking, taking about 10-12 minutes on medium heat.

Pancakes and Griddle Cakes

Cook pancakes on medium heat for about 2-3 minutes per side. Look for bubbles forming on the surface before flipping to ensure they are cooked through without burning.

Eggs

For scrambled eggs, cook on low to medium heat, stirring frequently, for about 2-3 minutes until they are just set. Fried eggs should be cooked for 2-3 minutes per side on medium heat, or until the whites are set and the yolks reach your desired level of doneness.

Bacon and Sausages

Bacon should be cooked on medium heat for about 4-5 minutes per side until crispy. Sausages typically need around 6-8 minutes per side on medium heat to ensure they are cooked through, with an internal temperature of 160°F for pork sausages.

Grilled Sandwiches and Panini

Grill sandwiches on medium heat for about 4-5 minutes per side, pressing down with a spatula or grill press to ensure even cooking and crispy bread.

Using these guidelines will help you master the timing of various foods on your griddle, ensuring everything is cooked to perfection and making your griddle cooking experiences consistently successful.

Griddle Meal Planning: Advice on Organizing Ingredients and Tools for a Streamlined Cooking Experience, Reducing Stress and Mess

Proper meal planning and organization can transform your griddle cooking from a chaotic task into a streamlined, enjoyable experience. Here are some expert tips to help you prepare effectively and reduce stress and mess.

Prep Ingredients in Advance
One of the most effective ways to streamline your griddle cooking is by prepping all your ingredients in advance. Chop vegetables, marinate meats, and measure out spices and sauces before you even turn on your griddle. Use small bowls or containers to keep everything organized and within easy reach. This not only saves time but also ensures you're not scrambling to find ingredients while cooking.

Use Mise en Place
Mise en place is a French culinary phrase that means "everything in its place." Arrange your prepped ingredients in the order they'll be used. This helps you cook more efficiently and reduces the likelihood of missing steps or ingredients. Having a clear layout of your ingredients makes the cooking process smoother and more enjoyable.

Organize Your Tools
Keep your essential griddle tools—like spatulas, tongs, and scrapers—close at hand. Use a utensil holder or magnetic strip to organize your tools and make them easily accessible. This minimizes the time spent searching for the right tool and allows you to focus on cooking.

Plan Your Cooking Sequence
Think about the cooking times of different ingredients and plan your sequence accordingly. Start with items that take the longest to cook, such as meats, and finish with quicker-cooking items like vegetables. This ensures that everything finishes cooking around the same time, so your meal is hot and ready to serve together.

Clean as You Go
Keep your workspace tidy by cleaning as you go. Have a garbage bowl or bag nearby for scraps and use your scraper to clean the griddle surface between different items. Wipe down surfaces and tools as you use them to prevent buildup and make the final cleanup easier.

Use Cooking Zones
Divide your griddle into cooking zones with different heat levels to cook multiple items simultaneously. For example, use high heat for searing meats, medium heat for vegetables, and low heat for keeping food warm. This strategy allows you to manage various components of your meal efficiently.

Batch Cooking
If you're cooking for a large group, consider batch cooking. Prepare and cook larger

quantities of each item, then keep them warm on the griddle or in a warming tray. This approach minimizes the stress of cooking multiple individual portions and ensures everyone gets served at the same time.

Stay Organized with a Checklist

Create a checklist of ingredients and tools needed for each recipe. This helps ensure you have everything ready and reduces the chances of forgetting something crucial. Review your checklist before you start cooking to confirm you have all necessary items on hand.

Utilize Storage Solutions

Invest in good storage solutions for your griddle accessories and ingredients. Clear containers, labeled jars, and stackable bins keep everything organized and easy to find. Efficient storage helps maintain a tidy workspace and saves time during meal prep.

Stay Calm and Enjoy the Process

Finally, remember to stay calm and enjoy the cooking process. Good organization reduces stress, but the ultimate goal is to have fun and create delicious meals. Take your time, enjoy the process, and don't be afraid to experiment and try new things.

By following these meal planning and organization tips, you can enhance your griddle cooking experience, making it more efficient, less stressful, and ultimately more enjoyable.

Advanced Cooking Techniques: Instructions on More Sophisticated Cooking Methods Such as Creating a Perfect Crust on Meat, Layering Flavors for Depth, and Using the Griddle for Baking

Elevate your griddle cooking skills with these advanced techniques, which include creating a perfect crust on meat, layering flavors for depth, and using the griddle for baking. These methods will help you achieve restaurant-quality results at home.

Creating a Perfect Crust on Meat

Achieving a perfect crust on meat adds texture and enhances flavor. Here's how to do it:

Dry the Meat: Pat your meat dry with paper towels before seasoning. Excess moisture prevents a good sear.

Season Generously: Apply a generous amount of salt and pepper, or your favorite dry rub, to the meat. The salt helps draw out moisture, which evaporates during cooking, leaving a flavorful crust.

High Heat: Preheat your griddle to high heat. A hot surface is crucial for creating a crust. Allow the griddle to reach the right temperature before adding the meat.

Use Oil: Apply a thin layer of high-smoke point oil, like avocado or grapeseed oil, to the griddle. This helps conduct heat and prevents sticking.

Sear Without Moving: Place the meat on the griddle and let it sear without moving it for several minutes. Moving the meat too soon can disrupt the formation of the crust.

Flip and Sear Again: Once a crust has formed, flip the meat and sear the other side. For thicker cuts, consider finishing in a lower heat zone to cook through without burning the crust.

Layering Flavors for Depth

Layering flavors involves building complexity in your dishes by adding ingredients at different stages of cooking. Here's how to master this technique:

Start with Aromatics: Begin by sautéing aromatics like onions, garlic, and ginger. These form the flavor base for many dishes.

Use Herbs and Spices: Add dried herbs and spices early in the cooking process to allow their flavors to develop. Fresh herbs can be added later for a burst of freshness.

Deglaze for Extra Flavor: After searing meat, deglaze the griddle with a liquid like wine, broth, or juice. This releases the flavorful browned bits (fond) stuck to the griddle and incorporates them into your dish.

Add Layers Gradually: Introduce ingredients in stages. For example, start with tougher vegetables like carrots and bell peppers, then add quicker-cooking items like zucchini and tomatoes.

Finish with Fresh Elements: Just before serving, add fresh ingredients like herbs, lemon juice, or a drizzle of olive oil to brighten the dish and add complexity.

Using the Griddle for Baking

Baking on a griddle is possible with the right techniques. Here's how to use your griddle for baking:

Temperature Control: Preheat the griddle to a moderate temperature, around 350°F, suitable for baking. Use an infrared thermometer to ensure even heat distribution.

Indirect Heat: Create an indirect heat zone by turning off one burner and placing the food over the unlit burner. This prevents direct exposure to high heat and mimics oven baking.

Cover with a Dome: Use a large metal bowl or a griddle dome to cover your baking item. This traps heat and creates an oven-like environment, allowing for even cooking.

Monitor Closely: Baking on a griddle requires close monitoring. Check the progress regularly to avoid burning and ensure even cooking.

Use Baking Mats or Pans: Silicone baking mats or cast iron pans can be placed on the griddle surface to bake items like cookies, flatbreads, or even cakes. These tools provide an even cooking surface and prevent sticking.

Example: Griddle-Baked Flatbread

Ingredients:

- 2 cups all-purpose flour
- 1 teaspoon baking powder
- 1/2 teaspoon salt
- 3/4 cup water
- 2 tablespoons olive oil

Preparation Steps: In a bowl, mix the flour, baking powder, and salt. Gradually add water and olive oil, mixing until a dough forms. Knead the dough for a few minutes until smooth. Divide into small balls and roll out into flatbreads. Preheat the griddle to 350°F and use an indirect heat zone. Place the flatbreads on the griddle and cover with a dome. Cook for 3-4 minutes on each side until golden brown and cooked through.

By mastering these advanced techniques, you can take your griddle cooking to new heights, creating dishes with professional-level flavor and texture.

Specialty Foods Preparation: How to Handle and Cook Specialty and Gourmet Foods Like Exotic Meats, Seafood Shells, and Artisanal Vegetables on a Griddle

Cooking specialty and gourmet foods on a griddle can be an exciting way to elevate your culinary skills. Here's how to handle and cook exotic meats, seafood shells, and artisanal vegetables on your griddle.

Exotic Meats

Exotic meats such as bison, ostrich, and venison offer unique flavors and can be a delightful change from traditional proteins. Here's how to prepare them:

Bison: Bison is leaner than beef, so it cooks faster and can dry out if overcooked. Season bison steaks simply with salt and pepper. Preheat your griddle to high heat and sear the steaks for about 3-4 minutes per side for medium-rare. Let them rest before serving to allow the juices to redistribute.

Ostrich: Ostrich meat is very lean and should be cooked quickly over high heat. Season with your favorite spices and cook ostrich steaks or fillets for 2-3 minutes per side on a hot griddle. Serve medium-rare to maintain tenderness.

Venison: Venison is rich and gamey, best cooked quickly to avoid drying out. Marinate venison steaks to add moisture. Preheat your griddle to medium-high heat and cook the steaks for 3-4 minutes per side for medium-rare. Let them rest before serving.

Seafood Shells

Cooking seafood like shrimp, scallops, and mussels on a griddle can be straightforward and delicious. Here's how to do it:

Shrimp: Shrimp cook quickly on a griddle. Season with olive oil, garlic, and your favorite spices. Preheat the griddle to medium-high heat and cook the shrimp for 2-3 minutes per side until pink and opaque. Avoid overcooking to keep them tender.

Scallops: Scallops need a hot griddle to achieve a perfect sear. Pat them dry and season with salt and pepper. Preheat the griddle to high heat and sear the scallops for about 2-3 minutes per side until golden brown. Serve immediately.

Mussels: Mussels can be cooked directly on the griddle or in a griddle-safe pan. Clean the mussels and discard any that are open and do not close when tapped. Place the mussels on the hot griddle and cover with a dome to steam. Cook for about 5-7 minutes until the shells open. Discard any mussels that do not open.

Artisanal Vegetables

Artisanal vegetables like heirloom tomatoes, purple carrots, and baby squash can add vibrant flavors and colors to your meals. Here's how to prepare them:

Heirloom Tomatoes: Heirloom tomatoes are best when slightly charred to enhance their natural sweetness. Slice them thickly, brush with olive oil, and season with salt and pepper. Preheat your griddle to medium-high heat and cook the tomato slices for 2-3 minutes per side until lightly charred.

Purple Carrots: Purple carrots are visually stunning and full of flavor. Slice them thinly or cut into sticks. Toss with olive oil, salt, and your favorite herbs. Preheat the griddle to medium heat and cook the carrots for about 8-10 minutes, turning occasionally until tender and caramelized.

Baby Squash: Baby squash are perfect for grilling whole or halved. Brush with olive oil and season with salt and pepper. Preheat the griddle to medium-high heat and cook the squash for 5-7 minutes, turning occasionally until tender and slightly charred.

Example: Grilled Exotic Meat and Vegetable Platter

Ingredients:

- 2 bison steaks
- 1 ostrich fillet

- 4 venison steaks
- 1 pound shrimp
- 1 pound scallops
- 2 heirloom tomatoes, sliced
- 4 purple carrots, sliced
- 8 baby squash, halved
- Olive oil, salt, pepper, and favorite herbs for seasoning

Preparation Steps: Preheat the griddle to high heat for meats and seafood, and medium-high heat for vegetables. Season the bison, ostrich, and venison steaks with salt and pepper. Cook the bison and venison steaks for 3-4 minutes per side, and the ostrich fillet for 2-3 minutes per side. For the shrimp and scallops, cook the shrimp for 2-3 minutes per side and the scallops for 2-3 minutes per side until golden brown. For the vegetables, brush with olive oil and season with salt and pepper. Grill the heirloom tomatoes for 2-3 minutes per side, the purple carrots for 8-10 minutes, and the baby squash for 5-7 minutes. Serve everything together for a stunning and flavorful meal.

By mastering these techniques, you can confidently handle and cook specialty and gourmet foods on your griddle, impressing your guests and elevating your culinary repertoire.

Seasonal Adjustments: Adjusting Griddle Cooking Techniques Based on Weather Conditions to Maintain Consistency in Taste and Texture

Cooking on a griddle can be affected by seasonal changes, from scorching summer heat to chilly winter days. Adjusting your techniques to accommodate these variations will help you maintain consistent results in taste and texture.

Summer Cooking

During the summer, high temperatures and increased humidity can affect your griddle cooking. Here's how to adjust your approach:

Manage Heat Levels: In hot weather, your griddle can heat up quickly and retain more heat. Monitor the temperature closely to avoid overheating. Start with lower heat settings and increase gradually as needed.

Hydrate and Oil: Food can dry out faster in high heat. Keep a spray bottle of water handy to add moisture to the griddle surface when needed. Use plenty of oil to prevent sticking and ensure even cooking.

Use a Wind Guard: Summer breezes can affect the flame and heat distribution. A wind guard helps protect the flame and maintain consistent cooking temperatures.

Plan for Quick Cooking: In hot weather, it's often best to prepare quick-cooking meals to minimize your time standing over the griddle. Focus on dishes like stir-fries, kebabs, and thinly sliced meats that cook quickly.

Winter Cooking

Cold temperatures can pose challenges, such as longer preheating times and maintaining consistent heat. Here's how to adapt:

Preheat Longer: Allow extra time for preheating the griddle in cold weather. It can take twice as long to reach the desired cooking temperature, so be patient and check with an infrared thermometer.

Insulate and Cover: Use a griddle cover or dome to help retain heat. This is especially useful when cooking items that require longer cooking times, like roasts or thick cuts of meat.

Wind Protection: Cold winds can quickly cool down your griddle. Set up a windbreak or position the griddle in a sheltered area to protect it from the wind.

Increase Heat Settings: Compensate for the cold by using higher heat settings. Keep an eye on the temperature and adjust as needed to maintain consistent cooking.

Spring and Fall Cooking

Milder temperatures in spring and fall provide a more consistent cooking environment, but fluctuations can still occur. Here's how to handle these transitional seasons:

Monitor Weather Changes: Spring and fall can have unpredictable weather. Keep an eye on the forecast and be prepared to adjust your cooking plans if temperatures suddenly drop or rise.

Maintain Consistency: These seasons are ideal for trying new recipes and techniques. Ensure consistent results by frequently checking the griddle temperature and adjusting the heat as needed.

Handle Moisture: Spring showers and autumn humidity can affect your griddle. Use a griddle cover to protect the surface when not in use, and be mindful of moisture when cooking. Pat food dry before placing it on the griddle to prevent excess steaming and ensure a good sear.

General Tips for All Seasons

Adjust Cooking Times: Seasonal temperature changes can affect cooking times. In hotter weather, foods may cook faster, while in colder weather, they may take longer. Adjust your timing accordingly to prevent undercooking or overcooking.

Keep Spare Fuel: Whether using propane or another fuel source, always have a spare tank or fuel supply on hand. Cold weather can cause propane tanks to freeze or perform less efficiently, and running out of fuel mid-cook can ruin your meal.

Stay Safe: Always prioritize safety, especially when cooking outdoors in extreme weather conditions. Ensure your griddle is on a stable, flat surface, and never leave it unattended.

Example: Adjusted Griddle Recipe for Seasonal Cooking

Griddled Chicken Kebabs

Ingredients:

- 1 pound chicken breast, cut into 1-inch cubes
- 2 bell peppers, cut into 1-inch pieces
- 1 red onion, cut into 1-inch pieces
- 1 zucchini, sliced
- Olive oil, salt, pepper, and favorite herbs for seasoning

Preparation Steps: In summer, preheat the griddle to medium-high heat. In winter, allow extra time to preheat and use higher heat settings. Thread the chicken and vegetables onto skewers. Drizzle with olive oil and season with salt, pepper, and herbs. In hot weather, cook the kebabs for about 8-10 minutes, turning frequently, until the chicken is cooked through. In cold weather, use a griddle dome to help retain heat and cook for about 12-15 minutes, turning frequently. Serve immediately.

By adjusting your griddle cooking techniques based on seasonal weather conditions, you can ensure your meals maintain consistent taste and texture, no matter the time of year.

Maintenance Pro Tips: Long-Term Care Strategies to Keep the Griddle in Optimal Condition, Including Seasonal Storage Tips and the Best Cleaning Products

Maintaining your griddle in top condition requires regular care and attention. These long-term care strategies will help you keep your griddle in optimal condition, ensuring it lasts for many years and delivers consistently great results.

Regular Cleaning Routine

Keeping your griddle clean after each use is crucial. Here's how to do it effectively:

After Each Use: While the griddle is still warm, use a griddle scraper to remove food particles and grease. Wipe down the surface with a damp cloth or paper towel. This prevents buildup and makes thorough cleaning easier.

Deep Cleaning: Periodically, perform a deep clean by heating the griddle and using a mixture of water and vinegar. Apply the solution to the griddle surface, let it steam and loosen any stubborn residues, then scrape and wipe clean. For tough stains, a specialized griddle cleaner can be very effective.

Best Cleaning Products:

- **Griddle Scraper**: Essential for removing food residues without damaging the surface.
- **Grill Stone or Scrubber**: Great for tackling tough, burnt-on grease.
- **Vinegar and Water Solution**: A natural and effective cleaning agent.
- **Griddle-Specific Cleaner**: Commercial cleaners designed specifically for griddles can be very effective for deep cleaning.

Seasoning the Griddle

Regular seasoning helps maintain a non-stick surface and protects your griddle from rust. Here's how to do it:

Initial Seasoning: Before using your griddle for the first time, wash it with soap and water, then dry thoroughly. Apply a thin layer of high-smoke point oil (such as avocado or grapeseed oil) to the entire surface. Heat the griddle on high until the oil starts to smoke, then turn off the heat and let it cool. Repeat this process 2-3 times.

Regular Seasoning: After each cleaning, apply a thin layer of oil to the griddle surface. This keeps it well-seasoned and protected from rust.

Seasonal Storage Tips

Proper storage is essential for keeping your griddle in good condition during periods of non-use. Here's how to prepare for seasonal storage:

Clean Thoroughly: Before storing, clean the griddle thoroughly to remove all food residues and grease. Season the surface with a thin layer of oil to protect it from moisture.

Protect from the Elements: If storing outdoors, use a durable, weather-resistant cover to protect the griddle from rain, snow, and UV rays. Ensure the cover fits snugly to prevent moisture from getting in.

Indoor Storage: If possible, store your griddle indoors during the off-season. This provides the best protection from the elements. Use a protective cover even when storing indoors to keep dust and dirt away.

Inspect and Maintain: Before storing, inspect the griddle for any signs of wear or damage. Tighten any loose screws or bolts and replace any damaged parts. Regular maintenance checks can prevent small issues from becoming major problems.

Preventing Rust

Rust is one of the biggest enemies of a griddle. Here's how to prevent it:

Keep It Dry: Moisture is the primary cause of rust. Always dry your griddle thoroughly after cleaning and apply a thin layer of oil to create a protective barrier.

Use a Cover: A good quality cover protects your griddle from moisture, dust, and other environmental factors that can lead to rust.

Store Properly: During long-term storage, ensure your griddle is in a dry, cool place. Avoid storing it directly on the ground where it might come into contact with moisture.

Regular Inspections: Periodically check your griddle for any signs of rust. If you find rust spots, clean them immediately with a grill stone or scrubber and re-season the griddle.

Maintenance of Griddle Accessories

Taking care of your griddle accessories ensures they last longer and perform well. Here's how:

Utensils: Clean your spatulas, tongs, and other tools after each use. Stainless steel and silicone utensils are dishwasher safe, but check manufacturer guidelines for specific care instructions.

Propane Tank: Inspect your propane tank and hoses regularly for leaks or damage. Replace any damaged parts immediately. During off-seasons, store propane tanks in a cool, dry place, away from direct sunlight.

Thermometers and Electronics: Clean electronic devices like thermometers with a damp cloth. Avoid submerging them in water. Replace batteries as needed and store them in a safe place when not in use.

By following these maintenance pro tips, you can keep your griddle in top condition, ensuring it delivers excellent performance for years to come. Regular cleaning, proper seasoning, careful storage, and routine inspections are key to prolonging the life of your griddle and maintaining its optimal functionality.

Quick Fixes: Handy Solutions for Common Cooking Mistakes and How to Salvage Dishes That Didn't Go as Planned

Even the most experienced griddle chefs encounter cooking mishaps from time to time. Here are some quick fixes for common cooking mistakes and tips on how to salvage dishes that didn't go as planned.

Overcooked meat can be dry and tough, but you can fix it by slicing the meat as thinly as possible against the grain. This makes it easier to chew and more enjoyable to eat. Adding moisture through a sauce or gravy, such as a broth-based sauce or a creamy dressing, can also enhance the flavor and texture. If you want to repurpose the overcooked meat, consider using it in a different dish like tacos, sandwiches, or a stir-fry, where additional ingredients can help mask the dryness.

If you discover that your meat is undercooked, simply return it to the griddle and cook it for a few more minutes until it reaches the desired doneness. Use a thermometer to check the internal temperature for accuracy. Covering the meat with a lid or griddle dome can help it cook more evenly and faster by trapping heat.

Burnt food can be unpleasant, but not all is lost. Carefully cut away the burnt sections of the food to salvage the remaining portions that might still taste good. For dishes like stir-fries or casseroles, mix in fresh ingredients to dilute the burnt flavor. Adding a strong sauce, such as barbecue sauce, creamy dressing, or robust gravy, can help mask any residual burnt taste.

Sticking food can be frustrating, but gently using a griddle scraper can loosen the stuck food without damaging the surface. Applying a bit more oil to the griddle surface can also help release the food. Ensure the griddle is properly preheated before cooking to prevent sticking in the future.

If your vegetables turn out soggy instead of crisp, increase the heat on the griddle to quickly evaporate excess moisture. Spread the vegetables out in a single layer to promote even cooking. You can also use a spatula to press out excess moisture or transfer the vegetables to a paper towel to drain. Giving the vegetables a quick sauté in a hot pan with a bit of oil can restore some of their crispness.

For bland food, add more seasoning such as salt, pepper, herbs, and spices, and taste as you go to avoid over-seasoning. Introducing a splash of lemon juice, vinegar, or a dash of hot sauce can brighten the flavors and add depth. Incorporating a flavorful sauce or dressing, like soy sauce, teriyaki sauce, or a homemade vinaigrette, can enhance the dish.

If your vegetables are undercooked, you can fix them without starting over by adding a bit of water to the griddle and covering the vegetables with a dome. The steam will help cook them through quickly. Alternatively, transfer the undercooked vegetables to a pan and sauté them with a bit of oil until they reach the desired tenderness.

When a dish is too salty, balance it out by adding more of the main ingredients to dilute the saltiness. For example, add more vegetables, rice, or meat. A splash of lemon juice or vinegar can help counteract the saltiness, and a small amount of sugar, honey, or a sweet ingredient like carrots can balance out the salt.

If burnt oil residue affects the flavor of your food, clean the griddle surface immediately after cooking with a scraper and a damp cloth to remove burnt residues. Always use fresh oil for each cooking session to avoid burnt flavors.

By using these quick fixes, you can salvage most cooking mishaps and still serve delicious meals. With a bit of creativity and flexibility, you can turn potential disasters into successful dishes.

Conclusion

Griddle cooking offers a unique and versatile way to prepare a wide range of delicious meals. From the joys and benefits of outdoor griddle cooking to mastering the art of using the Blackstone gas griddle, this guide has provided you with the knowledge and techniques needed to elevate your culinary skills.

Throughout the chapters, we explored everything from getting started with your griddle, understanding its components, and ensuring safety, to delving into basic and advanced cooking techniques. You've learned how to manage heat zones efficiently, use the right oils, and enhance flavors with marinades and wood chips. The troubleshooting tips and maintenance advice will help you keep your griddle in top condition for years to come.

The recipes section offered a diverse array of dishes, catering to various tastes and dietary preferences. Whether you're preparing quick weeknight dinners, hearty breakfasts, or gourmet feasts, the recipes provided are designed to inspire and delight. Specialty foods and seasonal adjustments ensure that your griddle cooking remains exciting and adaptable to any occasion or weather condition.

We also covered essential tools and accessories that can make your griddle cooking experience more efficient and enjoyable. By incorporating the recommended accessories and following the pro tips for long-term care, you can maximize the performance and lifespan of your griddle.

Finally, the bonus chapter equipped you with advanced techniques and quick fixes for common cooking mistakes, ensuring that you're prepared for any culinary challenge. By integrating these strategies into your cooking routine, you can create meals that are not only delicious but also consistently impressive.

As you continue your griddle cooking journey, remember to experiment with new recipes, flavors, and techniques. The versatility of the griddle provides endless possibilities for creativity and culinary exploration. Whether you're cooking for family, friends, or simply enjoying a meal outdoors, the skills and knowledge you've gained from this guide will serve you well.

Thank you for choosing this guide as your companion in mastering griddle cooking. Happy cooking, and may your griddle always be hot and your meals always be delicious!

Made in United States
Orlando, FL
08 December 2024